Fairytale *crochet*

D1148903

C015828385

Fairytale crochet

OVER 35 MAGICAL MINI MAKES

LOUISE TYLER

CICO BOOKS

LONDON NEW YORK

Published in 2014 by CICO Books
an imprint of Ryland Peters & Small Ltd
20–21 Jockey's Fields   341 E 116th St
London WC1R 4BW   New York, NY 10029

www.rylandpeters.com

10 9 8 7 6 5 4 3 2 1

Text © Louise Tyler 2014
Design, illlustration and photography © CICO Books 2014

The author's moral rights have been asserted.
All rights reserved. No part of this publication may be
reproduced, stored in a retrieval system, or transmitted in any
form or by any means, electronic, mechanical, photocopying, or
otherwise, without the prior permission of the publisher.

A CIP catalogue record for this book is available from the
British Library.

ISBN: 978-1-78249-147-7

Printed in China

Editors: Zoe Clements and Marie Clayton
Pattern checking: Zoe Clements
Designer: Emily Breen
Photographer: Martin Norris
Illustrator (steps): Kuo Kang Chen
Illustrator (backgrounds): Amy Louise Evans

In-house editor: Carmel Edmonds
Art director: Sally Powell
Production: Meskerem Behane
Publishing manager: Penny Craig
Publisher: Cindy Richards

For digital editions,
visit www.cicobooks.com/apps.php

Contents

Introduction

Once upon a time, in a little house by the sea, lived a woman who loved to crochet, knit and sew. She also had a passion for storytelling, fairytales and legends. One day she looked around her workroom and wondered how she could use up all the little scraps of fabric and yarn left over from her finished projects. She hated to see all these lovely supplies sitting idle so she sat in her comfiest chair and set about making lots of crochet items with a magical fairytale theme.

If all this sounds too good to be true you will have to forgive me a little artistic licence, but I hope you will allow yourself to be transported to a magical realm where yarn and hooks reign supreme. There are 38 charming projects in this book, each taking their inspiration from one of the favourite fairytales I read and listened to as a child. Some have a practical use but many are purely for decorative purposes. Most require only a basic working knowledge of crochet with an element of assembly to make the finished item. A confident beginner who likes a challenge would certainly be able to tackle almost everything, especially if, like me, they enjoy small, fiddly projects. If you make a mistake it does not mean you have to start again – in fact I largely use the crochet fabric to sculpt and mould three-dimensional objects and the crochet stitches themselves are really simple.

Telling yarns, tall stories and Chinese whispers...

I really wanted to make these projects inexpensive, quick, fun and a bit fiddly to make. As an avid consumer of crochet and knitting books, I have spent ages salivating over a project only to realize that it is going to cost a small fortune simply to purchase the yarn and fabric, let alone all the time spent actually making it. Invariably I don't even start! Or I attempt the project in different, cheaper materials that never really look or feel right.

These fairytale makes are much more forgiving. Most of them are made using DK yarn with my beloved 3mm (US D3) crochet hook, which generally gives a dense quality to the crochet that lends itself to being stuffed. Tension is unimportant here – if you wish to make the projects larger or smaller, simply swap the hook for a larger or smaller hook and use the corresponding yarn for the hook.

I am a bit of an off piste crocheter myself, and tend to turn mistakes into features. Unlike specific garment projects, there is really no right or wrong with these makes – in fact celebrate your own little changes, accidental or otherwise, because they will really give your pieces some individuality, character and personality. If it looks right to you then it is right! I call it 'go with the flow crochet'. Some may prefer the more structured, formal approach of other books, but others will enjoy the freedom to be creative that fairytale crochet brings.

Thrifty yarns

I am one of the world's worst yarn store customers – I often only buy one ball of a colour that I love and more often than not buy odd bits of yarn from charity shops and jumble sales. I am also fortunate to have good friends who donate oddments of yarn left over from their own projects. While I love beautiful luxurious silks, alpacas, cashmeres and merinos, these projects do not need expensive yarns to make them work. I have used DK pure cotton for a lot of the projects because it has a certain stiffness when made up. If you need to purchase yarn there are some really great acrylic mixes out there in lovely colours at affordable prices, but I am hoping that you can use up all those odds and ends of yarn that you can't bear to get rid of.

Remember that making these projects should be fun, not yarn-based torture. I would love you to be inspired to customize the patterns to make your own fairytale world, using the yarns and fabrics you have already, so if you want to use a chunkier or finer yarn just adjust the hook size correspondingly. This could be lots of fun… giant toadstool houses anyone?

Chapter 1

Princesses and Princes

Many traditional fairytales feature beautiful princesses and handsome princes who battle adversity and the odd storybook villain or two, then live happily ever after in royal wedded bliss. Here you will find Cinderella getting ready to go to the ball in her pumpkin carriage, Snow White and the seven dwarfs encountering a determined evil queen, and a small frog with royal connections waiting patiently for his princess to grant a magic kiss. Meanwhile, in an enchanted castle far far away, a bad fairy weaves a spell to make a beautiful princess sleep for a hundred years.

Skill level: ★★

Size

18cm (7¼in) tall

You will need

- DK (light worsted) yarn:
  Small amount of yellow or gold (A)
  20g (¾oz) of flesh tone (B)
  50g (1¾oz) of light blue (C)
  Small amount of silver metallic yarn (D)
- 3mm (US D/3) crochet hook
- Removable stitch marker
- Toy stuffing
- Tapestry needle
- Sewing needle
- Embroidery thread or 2ply yarn in black, blue, red and silver
- Silver or crystal beads (to fit the metallic yarn)

Abbreviations

alt	alternate
beg	beginning
ch	chain
cont	continue
dc	double crochet
dc2tog	double crochet two sts together
flo	front loop only
htr	half treble
htr2tog	half treble two sts together
rem	remaining
rep	repeat
ss	slip stitch
st(s)	stitch(es)
t-ch	turning chain
tr	treble

Cinderella Goes to the Ball

CINDERELLA

Cinderella's dearest wish comes true and her good fairy godmother works her magic. She wears a blue dress decorated with silver moons and stars, crystal and silver beading and a delicate coronet and crystal slippers made of silver metallic yarn.

BODY

Head:

Base ring: Using yarn B, ch5, ss into first ch to make a ring. Ch1, 8dc in ring, ss into first dc to join round. Place marker. Ensure you move the marker every round. Each round starts and finishes at centre back of figure, working in a spiral. (8 sts)

Round 1: 2dc in each st around. (16 sts)

Rounds 2–4: Dc around. (16 sts)

Round 5: [1dc, dc2tog, 1dc into next st] 4 times. (12 sts)

Round 6: Dc2tog to end of round. (6 sts)

Round 7: Dc around. (6 sts)

Fill head with toy stuffing. Turning chains are worked from this point on.

Increase for shoulders:

Round 8: 3ch (counts as 1tr now and throughout), 1tr at base of ch, 2tr in each st around, ss in 3rd ch of t-ch to join. (12 sts)

Round 9: Rep Round 8. (24 sts)

Fasten off yarn B and join yarn C.

Round 10: 1ch, [2dc, 2dc in next st, 3dc] 4 times, ss to first dc to join. (28 sts)

Bodice:

Round 11: 1ch, 4dc, miss 6 sts , 8dc, miss 6 sts, 4dc, ss to first dc to join. This creates two armholes of 6 sts each and a central bodice of 16 sts.

Cont to work into bodice sts only as follows:

Rounds 12–13: 1ch, dc around, ss to first dc to join. (16 sts)

Shape waist:

Round 14: 1ch, *4dc, 1dc, dc2tog, 1dc; rep from * once, ss to first dc to join. (14 sts)

Round 15: 1ch, 1dc, [2dc, dc2tog, 2dc] twice, 1dc, ss to first dc to join. (12 sts)

Crinoline skirt:

Round 16: 3ch, 1tr in base of ch, 2tr in next st, 1tr; [2tr in each of next 2 sts, 1tr] 3 times, ss in 3rd ch of t-ch to join. (20 sts)

Round 17: 3ch, [2tr in next st, 1tr] to last st, 2tr in last st, ss in 3rd ch of t-ch to join. (30 sts)

Round 18: 3ch, [2tr in next st, 1tr] to last st, 2tr, ss in 3rd ch of t-ch to join. (45 sts)

Rounds 19–23: 3ch, tr around, ss to 3rd ch of t-ch to join. (45 sts)

Work scallop edging:

Round 24: 1ch, dc in first st, * miss 1 st, 5tr in next st, miss 1 st, dc in next st; rep from * rep 10 more times, ss into first dc to join. You should have 11 scallops around the hem.
Fasten off yarn C. Weave in ends.

Arms:

Join yarn B to any st in armhole. Place st marker and work in spirals as follows:
Round 1: [2dc in next st, 2dc] twice. (8 sts)
Round 2: Dc around. (8 sts)
Round 3: [Dc2tog, 2dc] twice. (6 sts)
Rounds 4–7: Dc around. (6 sts)
Round 8: [Dc2tog, 1dc] twice. (4 sts)
Round 9: Dc around. Fasten off yarn B, leaving a 7.5cm (3in) tail. Use tapestry needle to weave into last round, tightening sts together as you sew.

Tip

When making the hair I also made a few stitches on the other side of the face in a curved line to make a curl, using the end of yarn A.

Weave in all ends.
Rep for second arm.

SKIRT BASE

Base ring: Using yarn C, 5ch, ss into first ch to make a ring, 3ch, 9tr into ring, ss into third ch of t-ch to join. (10 sts)
Round 1: 3ch, 1tr in base of ch, 2tr in each st around, ss in 3rd ch of t-ch to join. (20 sts)
Round 2: 3ch, 2tr in next st, [1tr, 2tr in next st] to end of round, ss in 3rd ch of t-ch to join. (30 sts)
Round 3: 3ch, 1tr, 2tr in next st, [2tr, 2tr in next st] to end of round, ss in 3rd ch of t-ch to join. (40 sts)
Fasten off, leaving 30cm (12in) tail.

FOOT

Using yarn B, 2ch, 4dc in second ch, ss into first dc to make a ring. Place marker. Move and replace marker as you go. (4 sts)
Rounds 1–4: Working in spirals (no t-chs), dc around.
Fasten off, leaving 10cm (4in) tail.

HAIR

Using A, 2ch, 8dc in second ch, ss in first dc to join. (8 sts)
Rounds 1–2: 1ch, dc around, ss in first dc to join. (8 sts)
Fill shape with a pea-sized ball of toy stuffing.
Round 3: 1ch, dc2tog to end of round, ss in first dc to join. (4 sts)
Rounds 4: 3ch, 1tr in base of ch, 2tr in each st around, ss in third ch of t-ch to join. (8 sts)
Round 5: Rep Round 4. (16 sts)

Quiff:

Row 1: 2ch (counts as 1htr), 5tr(flo), 1htr(flo), turn. (7 sts)
Row 2: 1ch, 1htr(flo), 3tr(flo), htr2tog(flo). (5 sts)
Fasten off yarn A, leaving a10cm (4in) tail.

SLIPPER

Using yarn D, 2ch, 6dc in 2nd ch from hook, ss in first dc to join. Place marker. (6 sts)
Rounds 1–3: Dc around. (6 sts)

Round 4: 3ch, 3tr, turn.
Round 5: 2ch, 3htr.
Fasten off. Weave in ends.

FINISHING

Fill body with toy stuffing. Thread yarn tail on Skirt Base into tapestry needle and stitch to base of skirt. Weave in ends. Sew foot to underside of scallop hem so it just peeps out under skirt at the front. Slide slipper onto Foot and sew in place.

Frilled neckline:

Using yarn C, 26ch, ss in first st to join.
[5ch, miss 1 st, dc in next st] around (13 loops in total).
Fasten off and use end to sew to neckline of bodice, starting and finishing at centre back st. Attach hair to head.

Ringlets:

Ringlet 1: Attach yarn A to any st at back of hair, 15ch, turn, work 1dc into each ch working back towards head, ss into join.
Ringlet 2: As for first ringlet, working 25 chains.
Fasten off. Weave in ends neatly.
The ch and dc braids will naturally coil into ringlets, but you can wrap the ringlet around your hook or a pencil to form a tighter ringlet shape if desired.

Coronet:

Using yarn D, 9ch, ss in next 3 ch, 1htr, 3tr in next ch, 1htr, ss into rem 3 ch.
Fasten off D, leaving 7.5cm (3in) yarn tail.
Push coronet over Cinderella's bun and stitch to bun with yarn tail. Weave in ends.

Embroidery:

Embroider face following the instructions on page 124 and using photograph as a guide. Use black thread for eyelashes, blue for eyes and red for lips. Chain stitch silver moons onto dress using silver embroidery thread or silver metallic yarn. Make straight stitch stars using silver thread. Stitch tiny silver beads to the bun and dress (see pages 122–123 for embroidery and beading stitches).

Skill level: ★★★

Size

15cm (6in) long
14cm (5½in) tall

You will need

- DK (light worsted) yarn:
  20g (¾oz) of burnt orange (A)
  10g (⅜oz) of green (B)
- 3mm (US D/3) crochet hook
- Tapestry needle
- Toy stuffing
- Felt – scraps of black, pink or blue
  and green
- Embroidery threads or 2ply yarn in
  colours to match the felt
- Oddment of gold yarn or small
  gold bead
- Medium gauge wire – four pieces 18cm
  (7in) long; two pieces 15cm (6in) long
- Small pliers
- 5cm (2in) diameter cotton reel or
  tubular shape
- 4 buttons 1cm (⅜in) diameter

Abbreviations

blo	back loop only
ch	chain
dc	double crochet
flo	front loop only
htr	half treble
rep	repeat
ss	slip stitch
st(s)	stitch(es)
t-ch	turning chain
tr	treble
tr2tog	treble two sts together
yrh	yarn round hook

Special abbreviation

Raised treble front (RtrF) – yrh, insert
hook behind stem of required stitch (from
front to back, right to left), yrh, pull up a
loop, yrh, pull through two loops (2 loops
on hook), yrh, pull through remaining two
loops to complete the stitch.

PUMPKIN CARRIAGE

This delightful crocheted pumpkin carriage with trailing leaves and wheels makes a lovely decoration. I have used raised treble stitch to mark the segments of the pumpkin, but you could work in trebles and then stitch on green lines at the end. There is an element of assembly to this project and – as with most of my patterns – you can customize it with your stash of ribbons, fabrics, beads and buttons.

PUMPKIN

Base ring: Using yarn A, 2ch (counts as 1htr now and throughout), 7htr in 2nd ch from hook, ss in 2nd ch of t-ch to join. (8 sts)

Round 1: 2ch, 1htr in base of ch, 2htr in each st around, ss in 2nd ch of t-ch to join. (16 sts)

Round 2: 3ch (counts as 1tr now and throughout), [1RtrF, 1tr(flo)] 7 times, 1RtrF, ss in 3rd ch of t-ch to join. (16 sts)

Round 3: 3ch, 1tr(flo) at base of ch, [1RtrF, 2tr(flo) in next st] 7 times, 1RtrF, ss in 3rd ch of t-ch to join. (24 sts)

Round 4: 3ch, 2tr(flo) in next st, 1RtrF, [1tr(flo), 2tr(flo) in next st, 1RtrF] 7 times, ss to 3rd ch of t-ch to join. (32 sts)

Round 5: 3ch, 1tr(flo), 2tr(flo) in next st, 1RtrF, [2tr(flo), 2tr(flo) in next st, 1RtrF] 7 times, ss in 3rd ch of t-ch to join. (40 sts)

Round 6: 3ch, 2tr(flo), 2tr(flo) in next st, 1RtrF, [3tr(flo), 2tr(flo) in next st, 1RtrF] 7 times, ss in 3rd ch of t-ch to join. (48 sts)

Round 7: 3ch, 3tr(flo), 2tr(flo) in next st, 1RtrF, [4tr(flo), 2tr(flo) in next st, 1RtrF] 7 times, ss in 3rd ch of t-ch to join. (56 sts)

Round 8: 3ch, 5tr(flo), 1RtrF, [6tr(flo), 1RtrF] 8 times, ss in 3rd ch of t-ch to join. (56 sts)
Start decreasing.

Round 9: 3ch, 3tr(flo), tr2tog(flo), 1RtrF, [4tr(flo), tr2tog(flo), 1RtrF] 7 times, ss in 3rd ch of t-ch to join round. (48 sts)

Round 10: 3ch, 2tr(flo), tr2tog(flo), 1RtrF, [3tr(flo), tr2tog(flo), 1RtrF] 7 times, ss in 3rd ch of t-ch to join round. (40 sts).

Round 11: 3ch, 1tr(flo), tr2tog(flo), 1RtrF, [2tr(flo), tr2tog(flo), 1RtrF] 7 times, ss in 3rd ch of t-ch to join round. (32 sts)

Round 12: 3ch, tr2tog(flo), 1RtrF, [1tr(flo), tr2tog(flo), 1RtrF] 7 times, ss in 3rd ch of t-ch to join round. (24 sts)

Round 13: 2ch, 1tr(flo) (counts as a tr2tog), 1RtrF, [tr2tog(flo), 1RtrF] 7 times, ss in 3rd ch of t-ch to join round. (16 sts)
Fill pumpkin shape with toy stuffing.

Round 14: 2ch, 1tr(flo), tr2tog(flo) 7 times, ss in 3rd ch of t-ch to join. (8 sts)
Fasten off yarn A, draw tail through remaining sts and tighten to close. Take needle and yarn through pumpkin to top of base ring, stitch through a couple of times easing the sphere into a rounded pumpkin shape.
Fasten off. Weave in ends.

Tips

If you prefer, you can stick the ends of the wire axles to the wheel with a glue gun, using an adhesive that will stick both metal and fabric.

As another option you could use four large buttons, each 5cm (2in) in diameter, as wheels instead.

STALK AND LEAF

Base ring: Using yarn B, 5ch, ss in first ch to join.
Round 1: 1ch, 12dc in ring, ss in first dc to join round. (12 sts)
Turn ring to WS and ss to centre. 16ch, ss in 2nd ch from hook, ss in each following ch to make a chain cord. Fasten off yarn B (leaving a long tail) and pull chain cord through centre of ring to RS.

Leaf:

Using yarn B, 8ch, ss in 2nd ch from hook, *1dc, 1htr, 1tr, 2tr in next ch, 1tr, 1htr, 1dc* 1ch, rep from * to * in other side of ch, ss in last ch. Fasten off yarn B. Use the tail to stitch leaf to stalk. Weave in ends.

FINISHING

Using yarn B, stitch stalk to centre top of pumpkin. Weave in ends.

Window and door:

Cut a piece of black felt and a piece of pink felt each about 2 x 3.5cm (¾ x 1⅜in). Matching up edges, cut one end of both pieces into a rounded or pointed shape. Place the black piece into the top of a pumpkin segment with the shaped end at the top and stitch in place using matching thread. Rep into the opposite (bottom) half of the segment with the pink piece, with the shaped end pointing down. Make a French knot (see page 122) with a snippet of gold yarn for a door handle, or stitch on a gold bead as desired.

WHEELS

Bend the shorter lengths of wire around the cotton reel or tubular shape to make four rings each measuring 5cm (2in) in diameter (use pliers if necessary). Twist the ends together and then tuck them tightly against the ring. Join yarn B to a wheel-frame and work dc around until covered, ss in first dc to join. Repeat to make 4 wheels.
Fasten off yarn B.

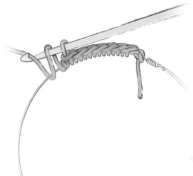

Spokes:

Thread the darning needle with a length of B and secure the end in the stitches covering the wire, draw the yarn across the centre of ring to the opposite side, secure again then weave along the covering stitches until you are an eighth way round. Repeat to create 8 spokes for the wheel. Cut 4 circles of green felt about 1cm (⅜in) diameter and stitch one over the crossed threads in the centre of each wheel.

Attaching the wheels:

Push the two longer lengths of medium gauge wire through the bottom of the pumpkin to make axles, making sure they are parallel and that the wheels will not block the door. Bend the wire outward slightly to make a better shape and trim the ends down to the position for the wheels, leaving a little extra to play with. On one side of carriage, bend both the ends of the axle into small loops, making sure the loops are big enough to draw a needle and yarn through. Leave the ends on the other side of the carriage straight for now as you will need to adjust the length of the axle when you attach the wheels.

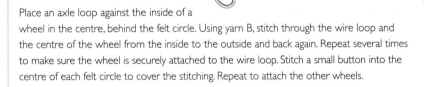

Place an axle loop against the inside of a wheel in the centre, behind the felt circle. Using yarn B, stitch through the wire loop and the centre of the wheel from the inside to the outside and back again. Repeat several times to make sure the wheel is securely attached to the wire loop. Stitch a small button into the centre of each felt circle to cover the stitching. Repeat to attach the other wheels.

Using a long end of yarn B and a tapestry needle, wrap yarn around the exposed wire of the axle, stitching through the wrappings at intervals to secure, until the wire is fully covered.

Skill level: ★★★

Size

15cm (6in) tall (nose to toe)

You will need

- DK (light worsted) yarn:
  10g (⅜oz) of white (A)
  Small amount of black (B)
  10g (⅜oz) each of pale blue (C), light
  brown (D), dark (royal) blue (E) and
  dark brown (F)
- 3mm (US D/3) crochet hook
- Removable stitch marker
- Toy stuffing
- Tapestry needle
- Pink, pale blue, royal blue and white
  sewing thread
- Sewing needle
- Medium gauge wire – six pieces 15cm
  (6in) long
- Pink felt – four pieces, 1cm (⅜in) square
- 6 silver or gold beads, 3mm (⅛in)
  diameter
- 7cm (2¾in) scrap of lace

Abbreviations

blo	back loop only
ch	chain
ch sp	chain space
cont	continue
dc	double crochet
dc2tog	double crochet two sts together
dtr	double treble
flo	front loop only
htr	half treble
inc	increase
pm	place marker
rem	remaining
ss	slip stitch
st(s)	stitch(es)
tr	treble
yrh	yarn round hook

WHITE MICE FOOTMEN

When the pumpkin is transformed into a carriage who can drive and be footman? Cinderella remembers the two white mice in the mousetrap; with a wave of the magic wand the mice are resplendent in fine blue livery ready to help Cinders get to the ball!

PIERRE MOUSE

Head:

Worked from the nose in a spiral.
Using yarn A, 2ch, 6dc, ss in 2nd dc to join, pm.
(6 sts)
Rounds 1–2: Dc around. (6 sts)
Round 3: [2dc in first st, 1dc] 3 times. (9 sts)
Rounds 4–5: Dc around. (9 sts)
Round 6: [2dc in first st, 2dc] 3 times. (12 sts)
Rounds 7–9: Dc around. (12 sts)

Ears:

Round 10: 5ch, 5dtr(flo) in next st, 4dc, 5ch, 5dtr(flo) in next st, 6dc. The dtrs form an ear on either side of the head.
Round 11: Working into back loops only of Round 9 (including the base of the st the ears were worked into), 9dc, leaving 3 sts unworked, turn. (9 sts)

Shaping back of head:

Work in rows as follows:
Row 12: 9dc, turn. (9 sts)
Row 13: Ss in first st, 1dc, 1htr, 3tr, 1htr, 1dc, ss in last st, turn.
Row 14: Rep Row 13, but do not turn. Cont to dc across rem 3 sts of Round 9 to join for mouse neck and work in spirals again. (12 sts)
Rows 15–16: Dc around. (12 sts)
Fasten off yarn A. Fill head with toy stuffing.

Body:

Place st marker in centre back of Row 16. Join yarn C at st marker.
Rounds 17–22: Dc around. (12 sts)
Round 23: [Ss in next st, 2dc , ch2, 1htr, 2ch, 2dc] twice. (12 sts and three 2-ch sps)
Fasten off yarn B.

Breeches:

Round 24: Attach yarn D at st marker, working in the stitches only (missing the chains) dc(blo) around. (12 sts)
Round 25: 2dc in each st around. (24 sts)
Round 26: Dc around. (24 sts)
Round 27: [3dc, 2dc in next st, 2dc] 4 times. (28 sts)
Round 28: Miss next 13 sts and insert hook into next st, yrh and draw through both loops on hook, 1dc in each of next 13 sts for first leg.
Work into first leg as follows:
Leg rounds 1–3: Dc around. (13 sts)
Leg round 4: 1dc, [dc2tog] 6 times. (7 sts)
Fasten off and rejoin yarn to first free st of Round 28 at other leg-hole, work 13dc, rep leg Rounds 1–4 for second leg.
Fasten off. Weave in ends.

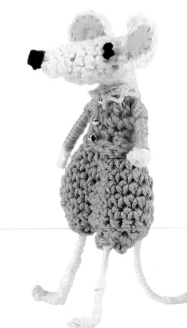

GUSTAV MOUSE

Head:

Work as for Pierre to Round 16.

Body:

Round 17: Using yarn E, dc around. (12 sts)

Round 18: [2dc in next st, 1dc] 6 times. (18 sts)

Rounds 19–22: Dc around. (18 sts)

Work flaps of jacket:

Round 23: 1ch, 4dc, 2dc in next st, 4dc. (10 sts)

Turn and work these 10 sts in rows as follows:

Rows 1–2: Dc across, turn. (10 sts)

Fasten off yarn E. Rejoin in first free st at centre front of Round 21.

Rep Rows 1–2.

Fasten off yarn E. Weave in ends.

Breeches:

Round 24: Join yarn F to centre back loops of Round 23, dc(blo) (under jacket flaps) around. (18 sts)

Round 25: Dc around. (18 sts)

Round 26: 2dc in first st, [2dc into next st, 3dc] 4 times, 2dc in last st. (24 sts)

Round 27: [3dc, 2dc in next st, 2dc] 4 times (28 sts)

Round 28: Miss next 13 sts and insert hook into next st, yrh and draw through both loops on hook, 1dc in each of next 13 sts for first leg.

Work into first leg as follows:

Leg rounds 1–3: Dc around. (13 sts)

Leg round 4: 1dc, [dc2tog] 6 times. (7 sts)

Fasten off and rejoin yarn to first free st of Round 28 at other leg-hole, work 13dc, rep leg Rounds 1–4 to make second leg.

Fasten off. Weave in ends.

FINISHING

Stuff body and breeches with toy stuffing.

Follow separate instructions on page 125 for making wire arms and legs.

For Pierre, use yarn C on the arms but yarn A on paw area and legs.

For Gustav, use yarn E to make sleeves and yarn B to make long black boots.

Join bottom of breech legs for both Pierre and Gustav.

Trim top edge of each piece of pink felt into rounded 'ear' shapes. Using appropriate colour thread, stitch one pink felt piece to each ear. Stitch 3 tiny silver or gold beads in a line down the centre of the jacket front for buttons. Pierre also has a little scrap of lace to make a fancy jabot collar, simply stitched in place.

Tail:

Wrap a 15cm (6in) piece of wire using yarn A, bending over ends and stitching in place as described for arms and legs (see page 125). Stitch through centre back of breeches to securely attach tail – you may have to wrap the yarn several more times and stitch through body several times to keep the tail from moving. Curl end into position to allow mice to stand up.

Tips

Make the two mice in matching colour livery if you prefer.

Use the stitch marker to keep track of the rounds and to mark where to begin and end.

"You shall go to the ball, Cinderella"

Size

19cm (7½in) tall

You will need

- DK (light worsted) yarn:
  20g (¾oz) of black (A), cream or ivory (B), white (D) and red (E)
  10g (⅜oz) each of lilac (C) and brown (F)
  Small amount of grass green
- 3mm (US D/3) crochet hook
- Removable stitch marker
- Tapestry needle
- Embroidery yarn in black and red
- 9 x 1.5cm (3½ x ⅝in) of brown felt
- Toy stuffing

Abbreviations

blo	back loop only
ch	chain
dc	double crochet
dc2tog	double crochet two sts together
flo	front loop only
htr	half treble
htr2tog	half treble two sts together
rem	remaining
rep	repeat
ss	slip stitch
st(s)	stitch(es)
t-ch	turning chain
tr	treble
WS	wrong side

Snow White and the Seven Dwarfs

SNOW WHITE

Snow White is truly the fairest in the land, with her jet-black hair, snow white skin, brown eyes, and rose red lips. She is worked using simple double and treble crochet. Her dress, with its red roses, laced bodice and lacy trim, is inspired by Russian folk costume and she wears a circlet of roses in her hair.

BODY

Worked from the top down; hair is made separately.

Make head:

Base ring: Using yarn B, 2ch, 12dc into 2nd ch from hook. Place marker. Ensure you move the marker every round. Each round starts and finishes at centre back of figure, working in a spiral. (12 sts)
Round 1: *1dc in next st, 2dc into next st; rep from * around. (18 sts)
Rounds 2–6: Dc around. (18 sts)
Fill head with toy stuffing. Turning chains are worked from this point on.
Round 7: 1ch, [dc2tog] 9 times. (9 sts)
Shape neck:
Round 8: *1dc, dc2tog: rep from *3 times. (6 sts)
Round 9: 1ch, dc around. (6 sts)
Increase for shoulders:
Round 10: 1ch, 2dc in each st around. (12 sts)
Round 11: 2ch (counts as 1htr), 2htr in each of next 10 sts, 1htr into last st. (22 sts)
Fasten off yarn B.

Make bodice:

Round 12: Join yarn C, 1ch, dc around. (22 sts)
Round 13: 1ch, *2dc in next st, 10dc, 2dc in last dc. (24 sts)

Make armholes:

Round 14: 1ch, 2dc in each of first 2 sts, leave next 7 sts unworked, 1dc in each of next 6 sts, leave next 7 sts unworked, 2dc in last 2 sts, creating two armholes of 7 sts and a bodice of 14 sts.
Round 15: 1ch, dc around central (bodice) 14 sts only. Fasten off yarn C.

Skirt:

Round 16: Join yarn D to base of bodice, 1ch, dc around. (14 sts)
Round 17: Ch3 (counts as 1tr now and throughout), [2tr in next 2 sts, 1tr] 4 times, 1tr, ss into 3rd ch of t-ch to join. (22 sts)
Round 18: 3ch, [1tr, 2tr in next 2 sts, 1tr] 5 times, 2tr into last st, ss in 3rd ch of t-ch to join. (33 sts)
Rounds 19–20: 3ch, tr around, ss into 3rd ch of t-ch to join. (33 sts)
Round 21: 3ch, 1tr in base of ch, 1tr, [2tr in next st, 1tr] 10 times, ss to 3rd ch of t-ch to join. (44 sts)
Fasten off yarn D.

Round 22: Join yarn C. Ch1, dc(blo) around, ss to first dc to join. (44 sts)

Rounds 23–24: 1ch, dc around, ss to first dc to join. (44 sts)

Fasten off yarn C.

Round 25: Join yarn E. 1ch, dc around, ss to first dc to join. (44 sts)

Fasten off yarn E and weave in all ends.

Picot edging:

Join yarn D. Turn to WS, 1ch, dc(flo) in next st, *ch3, ss in 3rd ch from hook, miss 1 st, dc in next st; rep from * around.

Fasten off yarn D and weave in ends.

SLEEVES AND HANDS

Attach yarn D to join of armhole and body. Place st marker and work in spirals as follows:

Set up round: 1ch, 3dc into the join, dc in remaining 6 armhole sts. (9 sts)

Rounds 1–7: Dc around. (9 sts)

Fill sleeve with toy stuffing.

Round 8: [Dc2tog, 1dc into next st] 3 times. (6 sts)

Round 9: [Dc2tog] twice, 2dc. (4 sts)

Fasten off yarn D.

Join yarn B with ss in any st, work dc in all sts for 2 rounds.

Fasten off yarn B, leaving a long tail. Thread tail into tapestry needle, stitch through sts of last round and tighten, st through hand and weave in end.

Rep for second arm.

SKIRT BASE

Base ring: Using yarn E, 5ch, join to 5th ch from hook with a ss, 3ch, 13tr into loop, ss in 3rd ch of t-ch to join into ring. (14 sts)

Round 1: 3ch, 1tr in base of ch, 2tr in each st around, ss in 3rd ch of t-ch to join. (28 sts)

Round 2: 3ch, [2tr in next st, 1tr in next st] 13 times, 2tr in last st, ss to 3rd ch of t-ch to join. (42 sts)

Fasten off yarn E, leaving a 30cm (12in) tail.

FOOT

(make 2)

Using yarn F, 2ch, 6dc in first ch, ss in first dc to join. Place marker.

Rounds 1–4: Dc in each st.

Round 5: Dc2tog to end of round. (3 sts)

Fasten off F, thread end into tapestry needle and draw through rem 3 sts to tighten.

HAIR

Base ring: Using yarn A, 3ch, 11tr into third ch from hook, ss into 3rd ch of t-ch to join into ring. (12 sts)

Round 1: 3ch, 2tr into each st to end, ss into 3rd ch to join round. (24 sts)

Round 2: Ss into each of next 2 sts, 2ch (counts as 1htr), 14tr, 1htr in next st, ss in next st. (16 sts) Leave rem 8 sts unworked.

Turn and work in rows as follows:

Row 1: 1ch (does not count as a st), 1htr in next st, 1tr in each of next 12 sts, htr2tog. (14 sts)

Row 2: 1ch (does not count as a st), 1htr in next st, 1tr in each of next 10 sts, htr2tog. (12 sts)

Rows 3–5: 3ch, tr across. (12 sts)

Fasten off yarn A.

FINISHING

Fill body and skirt with toy stuffing. Stitch base of skirt to inside of bottom of dress so Snow White stands up independently. Stitch foot to underside of skirt hem. Stitch hair to head.

Weave in ends.

Embroidery:

See page 124 for instructions for embroidering eyes and mouth, following the photograph as a guide for colours.

See pages 122–123 for embroidery stitch instructions. Using red embroidery thread work small French knots for roses on dress, spacing knots about 3tr apart around Round 22. Work chain stitch leaves in green yarn in a diagonal to rose. Work a chain stitch leaf between each rose on skirt.

For circlet roses, using red embroidery thread make bigger French knots (by wrapping yarn 4–5 times around needle), spacing 5 knots equally round head. Work a chain stitch leaf in green yarn between each rose on circlet.

CORSET

Wrap the small strip of brown felt around waist of dress, covering the centre rounds, and pin in place. Using yarn E, stitch bottom edges together leaving a small gap. Make a cross stitch above centre and secure with another stitch, then fasten off yarn E. Thread yarn E through top of corset above cross stitches, leaving a tail of about 7.5cm (3in) on either side of centre. Tie ends in a neat bow, tweaking loops until you are happy with the size of the bow, then trim ends off neatly.

Skill level: ★★ / ★★★

Size

11.5cm (4½in) tall (including pompom)

You will need

- DK (light worsted) yarn:
  20g (¾oz) each of blue (A) and brown (B)
  10g (⅜oz) each of flesh tone (C), Red (D), green (E) and black (F)
- 3mm (US D/3) crochet hook
- Removable stitch marker
- Tapestry needle
- Toy stuffing
- Embroidery thread or 2ply yarn in pink and black
- Ribbon for hanging loop (optional)

Abbreviations

blo	back loop only
ch	chain
cont	continue
dc	double crochet
dc2tog	double crochet two sts together
pm	place marker
rem	remaining
rep	repeat
RS	right side
ss	slip stitch
st(s)	stitches
tr	treble
WS	wrong side

SEVEN DWARFS

This little fellow is worked from the tip of his hat in a spiral, using a stitch marker and mostly double crochet. Make him in different colour combinations for seven different dwarfs or simply make him a solitary chap. He makes a cute hanging decoration especially if made in festive colours.

HAT

Base ring: Using yarn A, 5ch, ss in first ch to make a ring.

Round 1: 1ch, 6dc in ring, ss in first dc to join. (6 sts)

Rounds 2–3: Working in a spiral, pm, dc around. (6 sts)

Round 4: 2dc in each st around. (12 sts)

Round 5: [2dc in next st, 1dc] 6 times. (18 sts)

Round 6: Dc around.

Fasten off yarn A.

Fill hat with toy stuffing.

Hair:

The hair, face and beard are worked in separate sections. You can use a st marker at the start of each section but as the colours are different it should be easy to see where to work.

Round 7: Join yarn B at st marker, 1ch, 10dc(blo), turn (leaving rem 8 sts unworked). (10 sts)

Rows 1–2: 3ch, 9tr, turn.

Fasten off yarn B.

Face:

Row 1: Join yarn C to base of last tr worked. 1ch, 8dc(blo), ss in base of next tr, turn. (8 sts)

Rows 2–3: 1ch, dc across, around next tr to join, turn. (8 sts)

Row 4: 2dc, dc2tog, 2dc, ss in side of tr, turn. (5 sts)

Fasten off yarn C.

Tip

If you want your dwarf to have a hanging loop, stitch a 15cm (6in) loop of twine or ribbon to inside (WS) of hat and pull through centre ring to RS.

"Who's been lying on my bed?"

Tip

Make your dwarf with a white beard and red clothing instead to make a cute Santa Claus figure.

Beard:

Row 1: Join yarn B in ss, 1ch, dc across, turn.
Row 2: 3ch, 2tr in each of next 4 sts, 1tr. (10 sts)
Fasten off yarn B.
Fill head with toy stuffing.

Body:

Work along Row 1 of Hair section, in ss join and along Row 4 of face section (being 18 sts) as follows:
Round 1: Join yarn D at start of Row 1 (hair), 1dc(blo) in ss, 6dc(blo), 1dc(blo) in ss, 10dc(blo), pm. Work in a spiral from this point on. (18 sts)
Round 2: [2dc first st, 8dc] twice. (20 sts)
Rounds 3–7: Dc around.
Change to yarn D.
Round 8: Join yarn E, dc(blo) around. (20 sts)
Rounds 9–13: Dc around.
Change to yarn E.
Round 14: Dc around. (20 sts)
Fasten off.
Fill body with toy stuffing.

BASE

Base ring: Using yarn F, 5ch, ss in first ch to make a ring.
Round 1: 1ch, 12 dc in ring, ss in first dc to join. (12 sts)
Round 2: 1ch, 2dc in each st around, ss in first dc to join. (24 sts)

Feet:

Round 3: 3ch, 2tr in next st, 2dc, 3ch, 2tr in next st.
Fasten off yarn F.

FINISHING

Using yarn tails, darn sides of face, hair and beard if there are any gaps.
Place base inside body shape, with feet facing the front. Stitch base neatly in place.

Embroidery:

Using black thread or 2ply yarn make two French knots (see page 122) for eyes and a flesh-toned French knot in the centre of the face for a nose. You can leave the dwarf plain or you can stitch on buttons or beads to decorate.
Make six more dwarves, using different shades and types of yarn and customizing each one to give each dwarf a different personality.

Skill level: ★★★

Size

20cm (8in) tall

You will need

- DK (light worsted) yarn:
  Small amount of dark brown (A)
  20g (¾oz) of flesh pink or peach (B)
  30g (1oz) each of rich purple (C),
  bright red (D) and burgundy (E)
  Short length of black feathery or
  eyelash yarn (F)
  Small amounts of black and gold
  metallic yarns
  Small amount of green
- 3mm (US D/3) crochet hook
- Tapestry needle
- Removable stitch marker
- Toy stuffing
- Embroidery thread or 2ply yarn in
  red and black
- Tiny gold beads
- Paper and sticky tape

Abbreviations

ch	chain
cont	continue
dc	double crochet
dc2tog	double crochet two sts together
htr	half treble
pm	place marker
rem	remaining
ss	slip stitch
st(s)	stitch(es)
t-ch	turning chain
tr	treble
tr2tog	treble two sts together

EVIL QUEEN

Mirror, mirror, on the wall, who is the fairest one of all? My evil queen is truly beautiful in a sinister sort of way. Her cloak is trimmed with a feathery yarn to create a decadent garment and her sparkly crown is stiffened to make it stand up.

BODY

Worked in spirals, using a st marker to indicate end of rounds.

Head:

Round 1: Using yarn B, 2ch, 12dc in 2nd ch from hook, ss in first dc to join. (12 sts)
Round 2: Pm, 2dc in each st around. (24 sts)
Rounds 3–5: Dc around. (24 sts)
Round 6: [Dc2tog, 2dc] 8 times. (16 sts)
Round 8: Dc around.
Round 9: Dc2tog around. (8 sts)
Fill head with toy stuffing.
Shape neck and chest:
Round 10: Dc around. (8 sts)
Round 11: 2ch (counts as 1htr now and throughout), 1htr in base of ch, 2htr in each st around, ss in 2nd ch of t-ch to join. (16 sts)
Round 12: 2ch, 5tr, 1htr, leave rem 9 sts unworked.
Fasten off yarn B. Weave in ends.
Fill neck and chest with toy stuffing.

Dress:

From last st worked of Round 12, miss 4 sts, place st marker in next st (should be at centre back of figure).
Round 13: Join yarn C, 4dc, 2dc in each side of tr row in Round 12, 1dc in each tr, 2dc in side rows of tr, 5dc. (20 sts)
Round 14: [2dc, 2dc in next st, 2dc] 4 times. (24 sts)
Round 15: [2dc, 2dc in next st, 3dc] 4 times. (28 sts)

Shape armholes:
Round 16: 4dc, miss 6 sts, 8dc, miss 6 sts, 4dc, ss in first dc to join. This creates a central bodice of 16 sts and two armholes of 6 sts.

Bodice:

Rounds 17–18: 1dc into each st to end. (16 sts)
Shape waist and hips:
Round 19: [4dc, dc2tog] twice, 4dc. (14 sts)

Skirt:

Round 20: 3ch, 2tr in each of next 6 sts, 1tr, 2tr in each of next 6 sts, ss to 3rd ch of t-ch to join. (26 sts)
Rounds 21–24: 3ch, 1tr in base of ch, tr around, ss in 3rd ch of t-ch to join. (27 sts)
Round 25: 3ch, 1tr in base of ch, 1tr, [2tr in next st, 1tr] 12 times, 2tr in last st, ss to 3rd ch of t-ch to join. (40 sts)
Scallop pattern around hem:
Round 26: [5ch, miss 1, 2dc(flo)] 13 times, ss to first ch of t-ch to join. (13 chain loops)
Fasten off yarn C. Weave in ends.
Round 27: Join yarn D to any missed dc in Round 26, 3ch, 2tr in same st, miss one st, 1dc(blo) in next st (miss 1 st, 3tr in missed dc, miss 1 st, 1dc(blo) into next st) 12 times, ss to 3rd ch of t-ch to join. (13 tr scallops in between each of the chain loops)
Fasten off yarn D. Weave in ends.

"Looking glass upon the wall, Who is the fairest of them all?"

Sleeves:

Join yarn D to any free st of 6 armhole sts.

Round 1: [1dc, 2dc in next 2 sts] twice. (10 sts)

Rounds 2–3: Dc around. (10 sts)

Fasten off yarn D. Weave in ends.

Round 4: Join yarn C in any st, [1dc, dc2tog] 3 times, 1dc. (7 sts)

Rounds 5–8: Dc around.

Fasten off yarn C.

Hands:

Round 9: Join yarn B to any st, dc2tog, miss next st, 1dc into rem 4 sts. (5 sts)

Round 10: Dc around.

Round 11: [Dc2tog] twice, 1dc. (3 sts)

Fasten off yarn B, leaving a 10cm (4in) tail. Stitch tail through last 3 sts and tighten at tip of hand. Weave in ends.

Rep for other armhole.

SKIRT BASE

Base ring: Using yarn D, 5ch, ss in first ch to join.

Round 1: 3ch, 11tr in ring, ss in 3rd ch to join. (12 sts)

Round 2: 3ch, 1tr in base of ch, 2tr in each st around, ss in 3rd ch of t-ch to join. (24 sts)

Round 2: 3ch, 1tr in base of ch, [1tr into next st, 2tr into next st] 11 times, ss in 3rd ch of t-ch to join. (36 sts)

Fasten off yarn D, leaving a 25cm (10in) tail.

HAIR

Base ring: Using yarn A, 2ch, 12dc in 2nd ch from hook, ss in first dc to join. (12 sts)

Round 1: 3ch, 1tr in base of ch, 2tr in each st around, ss in 3rd ch of t-ch to join. (24 sts)

Shape widow's peak:

1dc, 1htr, [1tr, 1dtr, 1tr] in next st, 1htr, 1dc, (these sts make the pointed front of the Queen's hair) ss in next 3 sts, 3ch, 12tr, miss rem 3 sts. (21 sts worked)

To work back of hair:

Turn and cont in rows as follows:

Row 1: 3ch, 12tr, turn (leaving rem 11 sts unworked). (13 sts)

Row 2: Rep Row 1.

Row 3: 2ch, [tr2tog] twice, tr3tog, [tr2tog] twice, 1htr. (7 sts)

Fasten off.

FEATHER TRIMMED CLOAK

Base chain: Using yarn E, 15ch.

Row 1: 1tr in 4th ch from hook, 1tr in each ch across, turn. (12 sts)

Row 2: 3ch, 1tr in base of ch, 10tr, 2tr in last st, turn. (14 sts)

Row 3: 3ch, [2tr in next st, 3tr] 3 times, 2tr in last st, turn. (18 sts)

Rows 4–8: 3ch, tr across, turn.

Row 9: 3ch, tr2tog, 13tr, tr2tog. (16 sts)

Row 10: 3ch, tr2tog, 11tr, tr2tog. (14 sts)

Row 11: 3ch, tr2tog, 9tr, tr2tog. (12 sts)

Row 12: 3ch, [tr2tog] 6 times. (6 sts)

Row 13: 3ch, tr3tog, tr2tog. (3 sts)

Fasten off yarn E. Weave in ends.

Collar:

Rejoin yarn E at end of base ch. (12 ch)

Next row: 3ch, 1tr, 2tr in next st, 5tr, 2tr in next st, 3tr, turn. (14 sts)

Next row: 3ch, tr across.

Fasten off yarn E. Weave in ends.

Feather edging:

Join yarn F or any other fancy fluffy yarn (used double if needed) in side loop of last row, 1ch, 2dc in all side loops of rows around edge of cloak. Cont to work 1dc in each st, working 3dc in each corner. Cont around all sides, ss in first ch to join.

Fasten off. Weave in ends.

Fastening:

Fasten gold yarn to one end of base ch, 8ch, ss into other end of base ch.

Fasten off. Weave in ends.

FINISHING

Fill the body with toy stuffing.

Attach Skirt Base to skirt.

Using gold yarn, ch st around top of bodice and make a few decorative sts to embellish dress. Embroider face, following instructions on page 124 and using photograph as a guide for colours. Place cloak over queen's head, with gold chain under chin.

Crown:

Using black metallic yarn, 14ch.

Row 1: 1dc in 2nd ch from hook, dc in each ch across. (13 sts)

Row 2: 1ch, dc across.

Work crown points as follows:

[6ch, ss in 3rd ch from hook, 1dc in each of next 2 ch to return to main dc row, ss in next 2 sts] 6 times, ss to first ch of 6ch to join.

Make a tube from paper and tape. Fit crown over tube, spray with starch or a fabric stiffener and set aside to dry. When stiff and dry, stitch to top of Queen's head.

Tip

Eyelash yarn can be quite thin so it is a good idea to use it double to create a bolder edging.

You will need

- DK (light worsted) yarn:
  30g (1oz) of lime green (A)
  Scrap of yellow (B)
- Scrap of metallic gold
- 3mm (US D/3) crochet hook
- Removable stitch marker
- Toy stuffing
- Scrap of dark green or black
  embroidery thread or 2ply yarn
- Tapestry needle
- Fabric stiffener spray (optional)

Abbreviations

ch	chain
cont	continue
dc	double crochet
pm	place marker
rem	remaining
rep	repeat
ss	slip stitch
st(s)	stitch(es)
t-ch	turning chain
tr	treble
tr2tog	treble two sts together
yrh	yarn round hook

Special abbreviation

Bobble – yrh, insert hook in next st, yrh, pull up a loop, yrh, pull through two loops, *yrh, insert hook in same st, yrh, pull up a loop, yrh, pull through two loops; rep from *, yrh, draw through all loops.

The Frog Prince

FROG PRINCE

This cute little frog is worked in double crochet and trebles, again using a spiral technique and a stitch marker. You can position the legs how you like but I like him to sit down at the edge of the pond in the princess's garden. His golden crown is worked separately and attached afterwards and I have used a stiffening spray to keep it rigid.

HEAD AND BODY

(worked from top down)

Base chain: Using yarn A, 2ch, 8dc in 2nd ch from hook, ss in first dc to join. (8 sts)

Round 1: 3ch, 1tr in base of ch, 2tr in each st around, ss in 3rd ch of t-ch to join. (16 sts)

Round 2: 1ch, dc around, ss to first dc to join.

Round 3: 1ch, 10dc. Work eye by joining yarn B (leaving A attached at back of work) with a ss in next st, make bobble. Keep yarn B attached at back of work, switch to yarn A, 5dc, bring yarn B gently around the back of the fabric (and leaving A attached at back of work as before), make second bobble. Fasten off yarn B, switch to yarn A and dc to end, ss to first dc to join. (16 sts)

Round 4: 1ch, dc around, ss to first dc to join. (16 sts)

Fill head with toy stuffing.

Shape head:

Row 5: Pm, 1ch, 7dc, turn and work in rows leaving rem 9 sts unworked.

Row 6: 1ch, 7dc, turn.

Round 7: 1ch, dc around (including 9 sts previously unworked) ss in first dc to join. (16 sts)

Tips

I have used a spray stiffener to make the Crown rigid but if you are using cotton or wool yarn a spritz of spray starch should be fine.

For extra glitz you could also apply a little PVA glue to the crown and sprinkle gold glitter onto surface, shaking off all the excess.

Round 8: 1ch, dc around, ss in first dc to join. (16 sts)

Rounds 9–10: 3ch, tr around, ss in 3rd ch of t-ch to join.

Round 11: 3ch, 2tr in next st, 2tr, [1tr, 2tr in next st, 2tr] 3 times, ss in 3rd ch of t-ch to join. (20 sts)

Fill body with toy stuffing.

Round 12: 2ch, 1tr (counts as tr2tog), [tr2tog] 9 times. (10 sts)

Fasten off, leaving a long tail.

Thread tail into a darning needle and stitch through each st of the last round, tightening to close gap and weaving in end.

ARMS

(make 2)

Using yarn A, 8ch, turn, work 3dc back down ch, [4ch, work 3dc back down ch, ss in original ch, 1dc into next ch] twice, ss in last ch.

Fasten off, use ends to stitch arms to body at each side of shoulder. Weave in ends,

LEGS

(make 2)

Using yarn A, 2ch, 6dc in 2nd ch from hook, ss in first dc to join. (6 sts)

Round 1: Pm, dc around. (6 sts)

Round 2–9: Dc around. (6 sts)

Round 10: [1dc, miss 1 st] 3 times. (3 sts)

Toes:

Next round: 6ch, ss in 3rd ch from hook, [1tr, 3ch] 3 times.

FINISHING

Stitch legs to hip area of frog, bend into a sitting position and stitch ankles to body. Weave in ends of yarn and wrap round ankle and knee joint to accentuate the shape.

Crown:

Using gold yarn, 19ch, 1dc in 2nd ch from hook and each ch to end. (18 sts)

Work a pointed edge as follows, [5ch, 3dc] 5 times, 5ch, 2dc, ss to first ch in t-ch to join. (6 chain loops)

Join ends to make the crown shape.

Fasten off and stitch to frog's head.

Embroidery:

Using dark green or black embroidery thread or 2ply yarn, make a single horizontal stitch through each of the frog's eyes. Using chain stitch or a backstitch (see page 122) embroider a neat line for the mouth.

Skill level: ★★

Size
Pond: 17cm (6¾in) diameter
Flower: 8cm (3¼in) diameter
Lily pads: 7.5cm (3in) and 5cm
(2in) diameter

You will need
- DK (light worsted) yarn:
  25g (⅞oz) each of dark blue (A), light
  blue (B), medium blue (C), grass green
  (D), dark green E, white or pink (F)
  and yellow (G)
- Small amount of metallic gold
  yarn (H)
- 3mm (US D/3) crochet hook
- Removable stitch marker
- Tapestry needle
- Toy stuffing
- Embroidery thread or 2ply yarn
  in green or blue
- 14cm (5½in) circle of blue felt

Abbreviations
blo	back loop only
ch	chain
ch sp	chain space
dc	double crochet
dc2tog	double crochet two sts together
flo	front loop only
htr	half treble
pm	place marker
rep	repeat
RS	right side
ss	slip stitch
st(s)	stitch(es)
t-ch	turning chain
tr	treble
WS	wrong side
yrh	yarn round hook

WATER GARDEN WITH LILIES

The little frog prince wiles away the hours sitting by this little pond in the princess's garden, and he has just found the princess's golden ball! This water feature makes a charming setting with its water lilies and lily pads that the frog sits on.

POND

Base ring: Using yarn A, 5ch, ss in first ch to join.

Round 1: 3ch (counts as 1tr now and throughout), 1tr in ring, [3ch, 2tr in ring] 5 times, 3ch, ss in 3rd ch of t-ch to join.
Fasten off. (6 ch sps)

Round 2: Join yarn B in any ch sp, 3ch, 2tr in first ch sp, [2ch, 3tr in next ch sp] 5 times, 2ch, ss in 3rd ch of t-ch to join.
Fasten off. (6 ch sps)

Round 3: Join yarn A in any ch sp, 3ch, 2tr in ch sp, [2ch, 3tr in next ch sp] 5 times, 2ch, ss in 3rd ch of t-ch to join round. (36 sts)
Fasten off. (6 ch sps)

Round 4: Join yarn C in any ch sp, 3ch, 4tr in ch sp, [3ch, 5tr in next ch sp] 5 times, ss in 3rd ch of t-ch to join.
Fasten off. (6 ch sps)

Round 5: Join yarn B in any ch sp, 3ch, 4tr in ch sp, [2ch, miss 2 tr, 1tr, 2ch, miss 2 tr, 5tr in ch sp] 5 times, 2ch, miss 2 tr, 1tr, 2ch, miss 2 tr, ss in 3rd ch of t-ch to join.
Fasten off. (12 ch sps)

Round 6: Join yarn C in first ch sp after a tr group, 3ch, 4tr in same ch sp, 5tr in next ch sp, [2ch, miss 2 sts, 1tr, 2ch, miss 2 sts, 5tr in each of next 2 ch sps] 5 times, 2ch, miss 2 sts, 1tr, 2ch, miss 2 sts, ss to 3rd ch of t-ch to join.
Fasten off. (12 ch sps)

Round 7: Join yarn A in any ch sp, 3ch, 2tr in same ch sp, 3tr in next ch sp, 1tr in each st and 3tr in each ch sp around, ss in 3rd ch of t-ch to join.
Fasten off.
Turn to WS.

Round 7: Join yarn D to the flo of any st, 1ch, dc(flo) around, ss to first dc to join. Turn to RS.

Round 8: Work scallop pattern as follows:
1ch, [1dc, 1htr, 1tr, 2tr in each of next 2 sts, 1tr, 1htr, 1dc] 12 times. (12 scallops)
Fasten off yarn D, leaving a length of yarn to weave in. Weave in all loose ends.

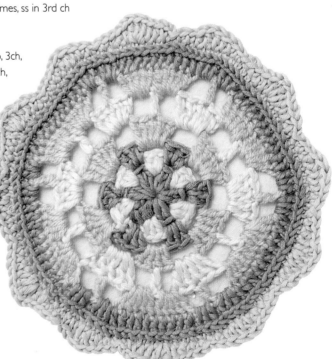

LARGE LILY PAD

Using yarn E, 3ch, 11htr in 3rd ch from hook, ss in 3rd ch of t-ch to join. (12 sts)

Round 1: 2ch, 2htr in next and each st around. Do not join, but leave round open, turn. (23 sts)

Round 2: 3ch, 1tr in base of ch, 2tr in each st around. Do not join. (46 sts)

Fasten off and weave in ends.

SMALLER LILY PAD

Using yarn E, 3ch, 11dc in 3rd ch from hook. Do not join, but leave round open. (12 sts)

Round 1: 2ch, 2htr in next and each st around. Do not join, but leave round open, turn. (23 sts)

Fasten off and weave in ends.

WATER LILY

Petals:

(make 6)

Using yarn F, 9ch, turn and work back along the chain as follows: 1dc in second ch from hook, 2htr in next ch, 2tr in each of next 4 ch, 2htr in next ch, 1dc in last ch, 1ch, rotate petal and rep into other side of ch, ss to first dc to join.

Fasten off yarn F, leaving a long tail.

Centre:

Base ring: Using yarn G, 2ch, 8dc in 2nd ch from hook, ss in blo of first dc to join. (8 sts)

Round 1: Work in the blo as follows: [6ch, ss in base of ch, ss in next st] 7 times. (eight 6-ch loops)

Round 2: Work in the flo as follows: Ss in flo of base ring, [3ch, ss in base of ch, ss in next st] 7 times. (eight 3-ch loops)

*Insert hook into the body of any dc from the base ring. Yrh, draw up a loop, [3ch, ss in base of ch, ss in next 2 sts] 4 times. (four 3 ch loops)

Fasten off G, leaving a long tail.

Attach the petals to the back of the water lily centre using the tail.

GOLDEN BALL

Using metallic gold yarn, 2ch, 6dc in 2nd ch from hook, ss in first dc join. (6 sts)

Place st marker in first st to mark the end of the round.

Round 2: 2dc in each st around. (12 sts)

Round 3–8: Dc around. (12 sts)

Fill shape with toy stuffing.

Round 9: [Dc2tog] 6 times. (6 sts)

Fasten off, leaving a long tail. Pull tail through 6 sts of last round to tighten, filling with more stuffing if required. Form into a ball shape and weave in ends.

FINISHING

Weave in ends.

Block pond gently if required.

On WS of pond, place and pin a circle of felt to the pond shape. Using green thread or 2ply yarn, blanket stitch (see page 123) the edges together to make the base sturdier.

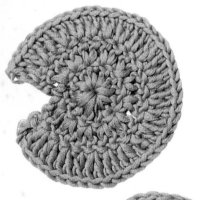

Skill level: ★

Size

14cm (5½in) tall

You will need

- DK (light worsted) yarn:
  20g (¾oz) each of dark green (A) and apple green (B)
  30g (1oz) of olive green (C)
  20g (¾oz) of pale cream (D)
  30g (1oz) of pale lime green (E)
- Small amount of fancy eyelash or feather type yarn in green (F) (optional)
- Medium gauge wire – six varied lengths measuring between 15cm (6in) and 25cm (10in) long
- 8cm (3¼in) ball of air-drying clay
- Green felt – two pieces 8cm (3¼in) diameter
- 3mm (US D/3) crochet hook
- Removable stitch marker
- Tapestry needle
- Pair of pliers
- Wire cutters

Abbreviations

beg	beginning
ch	chain
ch sp	chain space
dc	double crochet
dc2tog	double crochet two sts together
htr	half treble
pm	place marker
ss	slip stitch
st(s)	stitch (stitches)
t-ch	turning chain
tr	treble

WEEPING WILLOW TREE

This tree makes a delicate addition to your frog prince's garden. Made in the same way as the trees on pages 83 and 106, yarn is wrapped around the wire trunk and curling branches and crocheted, trailing fronds dangle down into the frog prince's pond. Use any oddments of fancy green yarn you have to add texture to the fronds.

GRASS

Work in the round, changing colour at beg of each round.

The fabric will form a curved dome shape as you work.

Base ring: Using yarn A, 6ch, ss in first ch to join.

Round 1: 5ch (counts as 1tr and 2ch), [2tr in ring, 2ch] 6 times, 1tr in ring, ss in 3rd ch of 5ch to join. (12 sts)

Round 2: Join yarn B to any ch sp. 5ch, [3tr in next ch sp, 2ch] 6 times, 2tr in last ch sp, ss in 3rd ch of 5ch to join. (18 sts)

Round 3: Join yarn C in any ch sp, 4ch, 1tr in centre tr of 3-tr group, 1ch, [3tr in next ch sp, 1ch, 1tr in centre tr of 3-tr group, 1ch] 5 times, 2tr in last ch sp, ss in 3rd ch of 5ch. (24 sts)

Round 4: Join yarn A in any ch sp before a 3-tr group, 6ch, [3tr in each of next 2 ch sps, 3ch] 5 times, 3tr in next ch sp, 2tr in next ch sp, ss in 3rd ch of 5ch to join round. (36 sts)

Round 5: Join yarn C to any ch sp, 3ch, 1tr in each st and ch around, ss in 3rd ch of t-ch to join. (57 sts)

Fasten off yarn C, leaving a 23cm (9in) tail.

WEEPING WILLOW LEAF FRONDS

Make tree as described on page 33. Each frond is worked separately.

To give the tree a natural look, it is a good idea to vary the length of the fronds and the amount of fronds coming from the top of each branch. I have also worked some plain chains along side the other fronds in a green eyelash yarn to give the willow an organic textured look. You can experiment with different yarns and chains to get the look that you want.

Work fronds as follows:

Using yarn E, *2ch, bringing yarn over hook from back to front, wrap yarn 5 times around first ch from hook, ss in 2nd ch (making a small bobble). Rep from * 11 more times, making a frond with 12 bobbles.

Fasten off yarn F, leaving a 12.5cm (5in) tail.

Use tails to stitch each frond to the end of each branch.

Make 18–20 more fronds of different lengths, (as a rough guide allow 3 fronds of different lengths for each branch). It gives the tree a more natural look to vary the length of the fronds and the amount of fronds from each branch, so feel free to customize as you wish, making more or less as you choose.

TREE

Place 6 lengths of wire together and twist together at one end to make a tree trunk. Leave the other ends free as these will form the branches.

Do not bend your branches into position at this point, as you will need to push the whole tree through the centre of the crochet and felt circles.

Base:

Roll a piece of clay into a ball shape and press down onto a tray or plate to flatten a base on one side. Mould the top into a rounded dome shape. Push the wire trunk into the clay to a depth of about 1.5cm (⅝in), take the wire out, leaving a trunk-sized hole, and set the clay aside to dry for 24 hours.

In the centre of one felt circle make a small slit with a pair of scissors to allow the wire trunk to go through. Using the tail of yarn C, stitch the crochet dome to the felt circle lining up the centre ring and slit in the felt circle.

Gently push the wire trunk through the centre of the crochet/felt piece. Put a drop of glue into the hole in the clay base and then insert the trunk into the hole. Ease the crochet/felt circle down over the clay base (see right) and allow the glue to dry.

When completely dry, stitch the second felt circle underneath the base using a length of yarn C.

Branches:

Using yarn D, stitch through the crochet base near to the wire trunk and start to wrap the yarn around the trunk from the base up towards the branches, stitching through the yarn occasionally to keep the wrappings in place. Continue to wrap around trunk until you reach the branches.

Bend the wire branches outwards and with pliers curl the ends over into spiral curls.

Wrap yarn around each branch in turn, stitching through the yarn to keep it in place as before until the branches are all fully covered in wrapped yarn. At the curled ends, stitch around and through any loops several times before cutting the yarn.

When all the branches are fully covered, bend the branches into magical, curling shapes.

"In a flash, the frog turned into a handsome prince"

Size

20cm (8in) tall

You will need

- DK (light worsted) yarn:
  10g (⅜oz) of dark brown (A)
  30g (1oz) each of flesh tone (B), pink (C), and white (D)
- 20g (¾oz) of silver ribbon yarn (E)
- 3mm (US D/3) crochet hook
- Tapestry needle
- Toy stuffing
- Medium gauge wire – 23cm (9in) length
- Black and red embroidery thread or 2ply yarn
- 5 pearl seed beads
- 2 pearl beads, 5mm (¼in)
- Small amount of silver embroidery thread
- White cotton thread
- Sewing needle

Abbreviations

blo	back loop only
ch	chain
ch sp	chain space
dc	double crochet
dc2tog	double crochet two sts together
flo	front loop only
htr	half treble
pm	place marker
rem	remaining
rep	repeat
ss	slip stitch
st(s)	stitch(es)
t-ch	turning chain
tr	treble

Sleeping Beauty

PRINCESS AURORA

Princess Aurora is a little bit different to the conventional princess character. To fit in with the style of the flapper fairies, this Aurora is a bobbed, twenties party girl complete with fringed dress and elegant T-bar shoes. It's just a shame that she is too tired to enjoy the party!

BODY

Head:

Worked in a spiral.

Round 1: Using yarn B, 2ch, 9dc in 2nd ch from hook, ss in first dc to join, pm. (9 sts)

Round 2: 2dc in each st around. (18 sts)

Rounds 3–8: Dc around. (18 sts)

Fill head with toy stuffing.

Neck:

Round 9: [Dc2tog] 8 times. (9 sts)

Round 10: Dc around. (9 sts)

Shoulders:

Work in rounds.

Round 11: 3ch (counts as 1tr now and throughout), tr around, ss in 3rd ch of t-ch to join. (9 sts)

Round 12: 3ch, 1tr in base of ch, 2tr in each st around, ss in 3rd ch to join. (18 sts)

Round 13: 3ch, 1tr in base of ch, 2tr, [2tr in next st, 2tr] 6 times, ss into 3rd ch to join round. (24 sts)

Armholes:

Work in spirals.

Round 14: 4dc, miss 4 sts, 8dc, miss 4 sts, 4dc. This creates two armholes of 4 sts each and a body of 16 sts. You will continue to work around these 16 sts in rounds.

Dress:

Round 15: Join yarn C at st marker, dc(flo) around. (16 sts)

Fasten off.

Round 16: Join yarn D, dc(blo) around.

Round 17: 3ch, tr round, ss in 3rd ch of t-ch to join. (16 sts)

Round 18: 3ch, 1tr in base of ch, [2tr in next st, 3tr] 3 times, ss in 3rd ch of t-ch to join. (20 sts)

Fasten off .

Round 19: Join yarn C at st marker. Dc(flo) around. (20 sts)

Fasten off.

Round 20: Join yarn D at st marker, dc(blo) around. (20 sts)

Round 21: 3ch, tr around, ss in 3rd ch of t-ch to join. (20 sts)

Round 22: 3ch, 1tr in base of ch, 4tr, [2tr in next st, 4tr] 3 times, ss in 3rd ch of t-ch to join. (24 sts)

Fasten off.

Fill with toy stuffing.

"The good fairies blessed the baby princess and gave her gifts"

SKIRT BASE

Base ring: Using yarn C, 2ch, 10dc in 2nd ch from hook, ss in first dc to join. (10 sts)

Round 1: 3ch, 1tr in base of ch, 2tr in each st around, ss in 3rd ch of t-ch to join round. (20 sts)

Round 2: 1ch, dc around, ss in first dc to join. (20 sts)

Fasten off.

ARMS

(make 2)

Round 1: Join yarn B with ss at armpit, pm, 2dc in join of armpit, dc around. (6 sts)

Rounds 2–5: Dc around. (6 sts)

Round 6: Dc2tog, 4dc. (5 sts)

Fasten off.

Gloves:

Rounds 7–11: Join yarn D at st marker, dc around. (5 sts)

Round 12: Dc2tog, 3dc. (4 sts)

Fasten off. Using tail, stitch through sts of Round 12, tightening them into a hand shape. Stitch centre of hand and weave in ends.

Rep into other armhole to make second arm.

LEGS

(make 2)

Base ring: Using yarn B, 2ch, 5dc in 2nd ch from hook, ss in first dc to join, pm. (5 sts)

Rounds 1–15: Dc around. (5 sts)

Fasten off.

Attaching legs to skirt:

Bend the wire into a U shape and push U shape into skirt base so that ends stick out of the centre. Bend ends into loops at each end to make feet. Place skirt base up inside dress and, using length of yarn C, stitch base to inside of skirt.

Place each wire leg carefully into each leg piece easing the foot loop gently to end of leg.

Using ends of yarn B, stitch the legs to the base of the skirt, stitching through base of skirt several times to secure.

Shoes:

Base ring: Using yarn C, 2ch, 6dc in 2nd ch from hook, ss in first dc to join. (6 sts)

Rounds 1–2: Dc around.

Heel:

Rows 1–3: 1ch, 4dc, turn, leaving rem 3 sts unworked. (4 sts)

Fasten off.

Rep for second shoe.

HAIR

Base ring: Using yarn A, 2ch, 9dc in 2nd ch from hook, ss in first dc to join. (9 sts)

Round 1: 3ch, 1tr in base of ch, 2tr in each st around, ss in 3rd ch of t-ch to join. (18 sts)

Round 2: 3ch, 1tr in base of ch, 2tr, [2tr in next st, 2tr] 5 times, ss in 3rd ch of t-ch to join. (24 sts)

Waves:

Round 3: 3ch, miss next st, 5tr in next st, miss next st, 19tr, turn. (25 sts)

Round 4: Ss in first 2 sts, [miss next st, 5tr in next st, miss next st, ss into next st] 4 times.
Fasten off.

FINISHING

Using tail of yarn A, stitch hair to top of head with waves at the back.

Silver fringing (dress):

Using yarn E, cut 36 lengths each 10cm (4in). Attach the tassels through the front loops only of Rounds 15 and 19 of the dress (the pink stripes) by inserting the hook into the loop, folding the yarn in half, pulling the folded end through the loop then taking the tails of the strands through the loop created by the ribbon yarn.
Trim ends neatly, so that fringes are even.

Headband:

Base chain: Using yarn D, 16ch.

Row 1: Ss in 2nd ch from hook, 3ch, ss in base of ch, 5ch, ss in base of ch, 3ch, ss in base of ch, dc in each ch to end, ss to first ch to join.
Fasten off.
Using white thread, stitch a pearl bead to band under the centre loop of 5ch.
Place the beaded loop at the centre front and stitch to head.

Shoes:

Slip foot into shoe and wrap end of yarn C around ankle, stitch through centre of shoe at front and make a large st that links to the ankle strap in a T-bar shape. Weave in ends.
Using white thread and sewing needle, stitch a tiny pearl seed bead to ankle strap at side of shoe.
Rep for second foot.

Shoulder straps:

Using a length of yarn C, embroider a line of 12 chain stitches (see page 122) from front of bodice, crossing over shoulder and ending on the other side of bodice at the back.
Rep on other side of the bodice to make two straps crossed at the back.

Embroidery:

See pages 122–123 for embroidery stitches and page 124 for making a face. With black embroidery thread, embroider eyes. With red embroidery thread, embroider the mouth. Remember to use sleepy eyes if you want a sleeping princess.
Using silver embroidery thread, work a few small stitches either side of the bead on the headband.

Bodice:

Using yarn C, make 3 long chain stitches in a fan shape in centre of chest, stitch a pearl bead to the chain stitch at centre and a smaller pearl seed bead to each of the other chain stitches.

Size

17cm (6¾in) tall (excluding feather)

You will need

- DK (light worsted) yarn:
  10g (⅜oz) of bronze (A)
  30g (1oz) of flesh tone (B)
  20g (¾oz) each of purple (C), black
  (D) and lilac (E)
- 3mm (US D/3) crochet hook
- Removable stitch marker
- Toy stuffing
- Tapestry needle
- Medium gauge wire – one 15cm (6in)
  length; one 20cm (8in) length; one
  7.5cm (3in) length
- Embroidery thread in black and pink
- Sewing needle
- Tiny amount of light brown yarn
- Small purple feather for headband
- Range of pretty metallic beads or
  fancy buttons in purple and silver to
  decorate fairy

Abbreviations

blo	back loop only
ch	chain
ch sp	chain space
cont	continue
dc	double crochet
dc2tog	double crochet two sts together
flo	front loop only
htr	half treble
pm	place marker
rem	remaining
rep	repeat
ss	slip stitch
st(s)	stitch(es)
t-ch	turning chain
tr	treble

BAD FAIRY

The bad fairy is, like her sister the good fairy (see page 40), free standing but if you want your fairy to fly, simply attach a ribbon loop to the top of her head, point her toes downwards and tilt her body. Remember, you can customize the pattern and decorations as much as you like.

HEAD AND BODY

Worked from top of head down.
Base ring: Using yarn B, 5ch, ss in first ch to join.
Round 1: 1ch, 9dc in ring, ss in first dc to join. (9 sts)
Round 2: 1ch, 2dc in each st around, ss in first dc to join. (18 sts)
Work in a spiral from now on.
Rounds 3–10: Pm, dc around. (18 sts)
Fill head with toy stuffing.

Neck:

Round 11: [Dc2tog] 9 times. (9 sts)
Round 12: Dc around. (9 sts)
Fasten off.
Round 13: Join yarn C at marker, dc around. (9 sts)

Body:

Work in rounds.
Round 14: 2ch (counts as 1htr now and throughout), 1htr in base of ch, 3htr, [2htr in next st, 3htr] twice, ss in 2nd ch of t-ch to join. (12 sts)
Round 15: 2ch, htr around, ss in 2nd ch of t-ch to join. (12 sts)
Round 16: 2ch, 1htr in base of ch, 1tr, [2htr in next st, 1htr] 5 times. (18 sts)
Fasten off.

Skirt:

First frill:

Round 17: Join yarn D in blo at st marker, 1ch, dc(blo) around, ss to first dc to join. (18 sts)
Round 18: 1ch, *1dc(flo), 5ch; rep from * around, ss final 5ch to first dc to join. (18 picots)
Fasten off.

Second frill:

Round 20: Join yarn E in flo at st marker, 3ch, [2tr in each of next 2 sts, 1tr, 2tr in each of next 2 sts] 5 times. (30 sts)
Fasten off.
Round 21: Decorative edge: Join yarn D at st marker, [3ch, ss in next 2 sts] around. (15 ch loops)
Fasten off.

BASE

Base ring: Using yarn C, 5ch, ss in first ch to join.
Round 1: 2ch (counts as 1htr), 11htr in ring, ss in 2nd ch to join. (12 sts)
Round 2: 3ch, 1tr in base of ch, 2tr in each st around, ss in 3rd ch of t-ch to join. (24 sts)
Fasten off.
Stuff body and attach base using yarn tail.

WINGS AND WAND

(make 2 lilac and 1 purple)
Base ring: Using yarn C or E, 5ch, ss in first ch to join.
Round 1: 1ch, *2dc in ring, 3ch; rep from * 4 more times, ss to first dc to join. (6 ch sps)
Round 2: 1ch, *3dc in next ch sp, 3ch, 3dc in same ch sp; rep from * in each ch sp around, ss to first dc to join. (6 star points)
Fasten off.

HEADBAND

Using yarn C, 33ch, ss in first ch to make a big loop.

Fasten off.

Flower:

Base ring: Using yarn D, 2ch, 6dc in 2nd ch from hook, ss in first dc to join.

Round 1: [3ch, ss into base of ch, ss into next st] 6 times. (6 petals)

Fasten off.

ARMS AND LEGS

Follow the instructions on page 125 to make the arms and hands, using yarn B for the hands, yarn C for the sleeves, and yarn B for the legs.

HAIR

Base ring: Using yarn A, 5ch, ss in first ch to join.

Round 1: 3ch, 11tr in ring, ss in 3rd ch to join. (12 sts)

Round 2: 3ch, 1tr in base of ch, 1tr, [2tr in next st, 1tr] 5 times, ss in 3rd ch of t-ch to join. (18 sts)

Shape hair:

Round 3: Peak at front:

1ch, 2dc, 1htr, 1tr, 3ch, ss in base of ch (at top of tr), 1tr, 1htr, 2dc (8 sts), pm, 3ch, 10tr, turn and work rest of hair in rows as follows:

Row 1: 3ch, 1tr in base of ch, 1tr, [2tr in next st, 1tr] 4 times, turn, leaving rem sts unworked. (15 sts)

Row 2: Bobbed shape:

5ch, 1tr, 1htr, 9dc, 1htr, 1tr, 1dtr.

Fasten off.

FINISHING

Using tail of yarn A, stitch hair to the top of head. Use tails of yarn E to sew the wings to the centre back.

Use black thread and sewing needle, stitch purple feather to the back of the flower, sew a few silver and purple sequins or beads to centre of flower and tail of yarn D to attach flower to headband.

Place headband onto head on top of head and position the flower and feather at the side of head, stitch in place using tail of yarn C.

Wand:

Make a small loop at each end of the 7.5cm (3in) length of wire. Wrap yarn A around wire until fully covered, stitch around and through loops at ends several times to secure.

Use yarn C to stitch the star shape to one end of the wire. Sew some purple sequins into the centre of star.

Stitch the wand to one of the hands and bend the arms into position.

Embroidery:

A delicate touch works best when working facial features, see embroidery stitches on pages 122–123 and instructions for making faces on page 124. Use black embroidery thread and a sewing needle to embroider eyes. Stitch eyebrows pointing down in the centre. Make a single stitch of light brown yarn to make the centre of each eye. Use pink embroidery thread to make a small cross stitch for a mouth.

Tip

You could use a fine permanent marker pen or a fabric pen to draw the eyes and mouth on if you prefer, instead of using embroidery.

Skill level: ★★★

Size

16.5cm (6½in) tall (excluding feather)

You will need

- DK (light worsted) yarn:
  10g (⅜oz) of gold (A)
  20g (¾oz) of flesh tone (B)
  20g (¾oz) each of medium pink (C),
  bright pink (D) and pale pink (E)
  Oddments of brown
- 3mm (US D/3) crochet hook
- Tapestry needle
- Removable stitch marker
- Toy stuffing
- Medium gauge wire – one 15cm (6in)
  length; one 20cm (8in) length; one
  7.5cm (3in) length
- Embroidery thread in black, light
  brown and pink
- Sewing needles
- Small pink feather for headband
- Range of pretty metallic beads or
  fancy buttons to decorate

Abbreviations

blo	back loop only
ch	chain
cont	continue
dc	double crochet
dc2tog	double crochet two sts together
htr	half treble
pm	place marker
rem	remaining
rep	repeat
ss	slip stitch
st(s)	stitch(es)
tr	treble
t-ch	turning chain

Special abbreviation

5ch picot – 5ch, ss in base of ch, rep as required.

GOOD FAIRY

It struck me that a true party-loving fairy would just love to dress up in true 'it' girl style and so my flapper fairy came into being. Use gorgeous ribbons, sparkly sequins, bright coloured feathers and tiny seed beads as extra decoration to make each fairy totally unique.

HEAD AND BODY

Worked from top down.
Base ring: Using yarn B, 5ch, ss in first ch to join.
Round 1: 1ch, 9dc in ring, ss in first dc to join. (9 sts)
Round 2: 1ch, 2dc in each st around, ss in first dc to join. (18 sts)
Rounds 3–10: Pm, dc around. (18 sts)
Fill head with toy stuffing.

Neck:

Rounds 11–12: Dc2tog around. (9 sts)
Fasten off.
Round 13: Join yarn C at st marker, dc around. (9 sts)

Body:

Round 14: 3ch (counts as 1tr now and throughout), 1tr in base of ch, 2tr, [2tr in next st, 2tr] twice, ss in 3rd ch of t-ch to join. (12 sts)
Round 15: 3ch, tr around, ss in 3rd ch of t-ch to join. (12 sts)
Round 16: 3ch, 1tr in base of ch, 1tr, [2tr in next st, 1tr] 5 times. (18 sts)
Fasten off.

Skirt frills:

Round 17: Join yarn A in blo at st marker, [ss in next st, 3tr in next st, ss in next st] 6 times. (6 scallops)
Fasten off.
Round 18: Join yarn D at st marker, working in the same blo of Round 16 1ch, dc(blo) around. (18 sts)

Round 19: 1ch, 2dc, [2dc in next st, 2dc] 5 times, 2dc in next st, ss in first dc to join. (24 sts)
Round 20: [5ch, ss in base of ch, ss in next 2 sts] 12 times, ss in base of first 5ch picot worked to join. (12 picots)
Fasten off.

Tutu:

Row 1: Using yarn E, 26ch, 1tr in 4th ch from hook, 1tr in each ch across. (23 sts)
Frilled edge:
Row 2: *[3ch, ss in base of ch, 5ch, ss in base of ch, 3ch, ss in base of ch] ss in next 2 sts; rep from * 11 times, [3ch, ss in base of ch, 5ch, ss in base of ch, 3ch, ss in base of ch] in last st. (12 frills)
Fasten off.

BASE

Base ring: Using yarn C , 5ch, ss in first ch to join.
Round 1: 2ch (counts as 1htr now and throughout), 11htr in ring, ss in second ch of t-ch to join. (12 sts)
Round 2: 3ch, 1tr in base of ch, 2tr in each st around, ss in 3rd ch of t-ch to join. (24 sts)
Fasten off.
Stuff body and attach base using yarn tail.

WINGS

(make 2)
Row 1: Using yarn E, 7ch, 1dc in 2nd ch from hook, dc in each ch across. (6 sts)
Row 2: 3ch, 2tr in next st, miss next st, 3dtr in next st, miss next st, 3tr in next st.
Fasten off.
Re-attach yarn E to side of base ch and rep Row 2 to make second wing.
Fasten off.

HEADBAND

Using yarn C, 33ch, ss in first ch to make a loop.
Fasten off.

Flower:

Base ring: Using yarn D, 2ch, 6dc in 2nd ch from hook, ss in first dc to join. (6 sts)
Round 1: [3ch, ss in base of ch, ss in next st] 5 times, 3ch, ss to base of first 3ch to join. (6 petals)
Fasten off.

STAR FOR WAND

Base ring: Using yarn D, 5ch, ss in first ch to join.
Round 1: 1ch, *2dc in ring, 3ch; rep from * 6 times, ss to first dc to join. (6 points)
Round 2: [2dc in next ch sp, 3ch, 2dc in same ch sp] around, ss to first dc to join. (6 point star)
Fasten off.

HAIR

Base ring: Using yarn A, 5ch, ss in first ch to join.
Round 1: 3ch, 11tr in ring, ss in 3rd ch of t-ch to join. (12 sts)
Round 2: 3ch, 1tr in base of ch, 1tr, [2tr in next st, 1tr] 5 times, ss in 3rd ch of t-ch to join. (18 sts)
Round 3: 3ch, 11tr, turn and work in rows, leaving rem 6 sts unworked, as follows:
Row 1: 3ch, 11tr, turn. (12 sts)
Row 2: 2ch, 11htr, turn. (12 sts)

Curls:

Work into all sts around, including the sides of the tr and htr rows (working one rep per row) where required as follows:
*3ch, ss in next 2 sts; rep from * around.
Fasten off.
You will have 15 chain loop curls.

ARMS AND LEGS

Follow the instructions on page 125 to make the arms and hands, using yarn B for the hands, yarn C for the sleeves, and yarn B for the legs.

FINISHING

Using tail of yarn A, stitch hair to the top of head. Use yarn E to sew the wings to the centre back of figure.
Using pink thread and sewing needle, stitch pink feather to the back of the flower, sew a few gold and pink beads into centre of flower and using tail of yarn D attach flower to headband.
Place headband on top of head and position the flower and feather at the side, stitch in place using tail of yarn C.

Wand:

Make a small loop at each end of the 7.5cm (3in) length of wire. Use yarn A to wrap around wire until fully covered, stitch around and through loops at ends several times to secure.
Using yarn D, stitch the star shape to one end of the wire, with pink thread and sewing needle, sew some gold sequins into the centre of star. Stitch the wand to one of the hands and bend the arms into position.

Embroidery:

A delicate touch works best when working facial features, see embroidery stitches on pages 122–123 and instructions for making faces on page 124. Use black embroidery thread and a sewing needle to embroider eyes. Make a single stitch of brown yarn to make the centre of each eye. Use light brown embroidery thread to make rounded eyebrows. Use pink embroidery thread to make a small cross stitch for a mouth.

Size

Height: 20cm (8in) to highest turret
Base: 10 x 12.5cm (4 x 5in)

You will need

- DK (light worsted) yarn:
  50g (1¾oz) of light grey (A)
  30g (1oz) of darker grey (B)
  Oddments of dark brown (C)
- 3mm (US D/3) crochet hook
- Removable stitch marker
- Tapestry needle
- Toy stuffing
- Black/navy felt – 3.5cm (1⅜in) square;
  six 1cm (⅜in) squares
- Pale pink felt – three equilateral 1cm
  (⅜in) triangles
- Green felt – two 1.5cm (⅝in) circles
- Bright pink felt – 1 x 6cm (⅜ x 2⅜in)
  piece
- Orange felt – 1 x 6cm (⅜ x 2⅜in)
  piece
- 2 cocktail sticks
- Thin card – four 11 x 7cm (4⅜ x 2¾in)
  rectangles; two 10 x 7cm (4 x 2¾in)
  rectangles
- Embroidery threads in black, cream
  and green
- Pretty buttons, sequins and ribbons of
  choice to decorate the castle
- Sewing needle

Abbreviations

blo	back loop only
ch	chain
dc	double crochet
rem	remaining
ss	slip stitch
st(s)	stitch(es)
t-ch	turning chain
tr	treble

FAIRYTALE CASTLE

This bijou royal retreat can be used as a background piece to many of the fairytales. The castle is made in separate pieces using rectangles of treble crochet for the castle walls, base and roof. The turrets are made in spirals of double crochet then all the pieces are stitched together at the end. You will need to stiffen the sides, roof and base with a little cardboard or iron-on interfacing. You can go to town on the decoration, making the castle as opulent as you wish – again a good excuse for using up trimmings and haberdashery that you have left over from previous projects.

BASE AND ROOF

(make 2)
Base chain: Using yarn A, 27ch.
Row 1: 1tr into 4th ch from hook, 1tr into each ch to end of row, turn. (24 sts)
Rows 2–10: 3ch (counts as 1tr now and throughout), tr across, turn. (24 sts)
Fasten off A, leaving a 20cm (8in) tail.

Front and back:

(make 2)
Rows 1–7: Work as for Base and Roof.

Crenellations:

Row 8: Ss into next st, *3ch, 2tr, 3ch, ss in base of last tr worked, ss across next 3 sts; rep from * 4 times, ss to last st. (5 crenellations along row)
Fasten off yarn A, leaving a 20cm (8in) tail.

SIDES

(make 2)
Base chain: Using yarn A, 23ch.
Row 1: 1tr into 4th ch from hook, 1tr in each ch to end of row. (20 sts)
Rows 2–7: 3ch, 1tr into second st (from hook), 1tr into rem sts to end of row, turn.

Crenellations:

Row 8: *3ch, 1tr into each of next 2 sts, ch3 (from top of last tr) ss into base of last tr made, ss across next 3 sts; * rep from * 3 more times. (4 crenellations along row)
Fasten off yarn A, leaving a 20cm (8in) tail.

TOWERS

(make 5 separately in different heights)
Each tower is made in two sections and stitched together. It is easier to make all the pieces first, then stitch them all together at the end.

Tall turret:

(make 1)
Worked in a spiral from top down, moving st marker as you work.
Base ring: Using yarn B, 2ch, 6dc in second ch from hook, ss into first dc to join. (6 sts)
Rounds 1–3: Dc around. (6 sts)
Round 4: [2dc in next st, 1dc] 3 times. (9 sts)
Rounds 5–6: Dc across. (9 sts)
Round 7: [2dc in next st, 1dc] 4 times, 2dc in last st. (14 sts)
Rounds 8–12: 1dc, [2dc in next st, 3dc] 3 times, 2dc into last st. (18 sts)
Rounds 12–14: Dc around. Ss in first dc to join at end of Round 14. (18 sts)
Fasten off.

Tall tower:

(make 1)

Worked from base up.

Base ring: Using yarn A, 5ch, ss in first ch to join.

Round 1: 1ch, 8dc in ring, ss in first dc to join. Place st marker. (8 sts)

Round 2: 3ch (counts as 1tr now and throughout), 1tr in base of ch, 2tr in each st around, ss into 3rd ch of t-ch to join. (16 sts)

Round 3: 1ch, 1dc(blo) around, ss in first dc to join. (16 sts)

Rounds 4–18: Dc around, in a spiral (no t-ch or joins). Ss into first dc to join at end of last round. Fasten off yarn A, leaving a 7.5cm (3in) tail.

Medium turrets:

(make 2)

Work as for tall turret to Round 12.

Fasten off yarn B, leaving a 7.5cm (3in) tail.

Medium tower:

(make 2)

Worked from base up.

Base ring: Using yarn A, 5ch, ss into 5th ch from hook to join.

Round 1: 1ch, 8dc in ring, ss in first dc to join. Place st marker. (8 sts)

Round 2: 3ch, 1tr in base of ch, 2tr in each st around, ss in 3rd ch of t-ch to join. (16 sts)

Round 3: 1ch, 1dc(blo) around, ss in first dc to join. (16 sts)

Rounds 4–12: Dc around, in a spiral. Ss in first dc to join at end of last round.

Fasten off yarn A, leaving a 7.5cm (3in) tail.

Small turret:

(make 1)

Work as for tall turret to Round 12.

Fasten off yarn B, leaving a 7.5cm (3in) tail.

Small tower:

(make 1)

Working from base up as before.

Base ring: Using yarn A, 5ch, ss into first ch to join.

Round 1: 3ch, 13tr in ring, ss in 3rd ch of t-ch to join. Place st marker. (14 sts)

Round 2: 1ch, 1dc(blo) around, ss in first dc to join. (14 sts)

Rounds 3–10: Dc around, in a spiral. Ss in first dc to join at end of last round.

Fasten off yarn A, leaving a 7.5cm (3in) tail.

Short central turret:

(make 1)

Worked in a spiral from top down.

Base ring: Using yarn B, 2ch, 6dc in 2nd ch from hook, ss in first dc to join. Place marker. (6 sts)

Rounds 1–4: Dc around. (6 sts)

Rounds 5: 2dc in each st around. (12 sts)

Round 7: [2dc in next st, 5dc] twice. (14 sts)

Round 8: Dc around. (14 sts)

Round 9: 2dc in each st around. (28 sts)

Round 10: Dc around, ss in first dc to join. (28 sts)

Short central tower:

(make 1)

Working from base up as before.

Base ring: Using yarn A, 5ch, ss in 5th ch from hook to join.

Round 1: 3ch, 9tr into ring, ss in 3rd ch of t-ch to join. (10 sts)

Round 2: 3ch, 1tr in base of ch, 2tr in each st around, ss in 3rd ch of t-ch to join. (20 sts)

Round 3: 1ch, dc around, ss in first dc to join. (20 sts)

Rounds 4–11: Dc around, in a spiral. Ss in first dc to join at end of last round.

Fasten off yarn A, leaving a 7.5cm (3in) tail.

CONSTRUCTION
Towers and turrets:

Fill each turret and base of tower with toy stuffing and stitch each turret to top of its tower using tails of yarn B and tapestry needle.

Castle shape:

Using a length of yarn A and tapestry needle, stitch the cardboard pieces lightly to the wrong side of each crochet rectangle (front, back and sides). Or iron on fusible interfacing to support the shape. Using tails of yarn A, stitch the base to front, back and sides so that you have a box shape. Fill the box shape with toy stuffing, stitch the roof piece to the top of the box shape below the crenellations (see diagram 1).

Using yarn A and tapestry needle, stitch the short central tower into the centre of roof rectangle, stitch the tall tower behind the short

1.

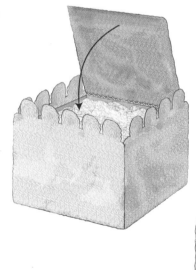

2.

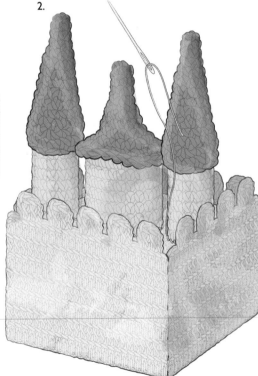

central tower at the centre back of castle. Stitch the two medium-sized towers to each corner of the roof at the left-hand side of castle, stitch remaining small tower at the centre of the other side of the roof (see diagram 2). You can arrange the towers anywhere you like and even add more towers and turrets if you wish. Keep checking the position of the towers on the main castle keep while you work to ensure that they look correct when put in place. A certain amount of tweaking can then be done as you work to make the towers look right for your individual castle.

3.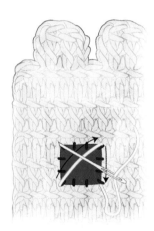

4.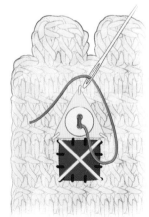

FINISHING

Take the 3.5cm (1⅜in) rectangle of black or navy felt and cut one end into a pointed shape to make a door.

Using black embroidery thread and sewing needle, sew the door to the centre front of the castle at the bottom edge.

Windows:

Using black embroidery thread and sewing needle, stitch the windows either side of the door at about Row 4. If you prefer, you can glue the felt windows instead of stitching them on. Make sure that you use glue suitable for fabric and follow the manufacturer's instructions, allowing plenty of time for it to dry. With cream embroidery thread make two cross stitches across each window (see diagram 3).

Stitch a window to the tall turret and the smaller turret, sew one window to each tower. Stitch the pink triangles above each side window on the castle and above the window on the tall tower. With black embroidery thread, sew a small button into the centre of each triangle (see diagram 4).

Decoration:

Using green embroidery thread and sewing needle, stitch the two circles of green felt under the windows at the front of the castle. Make a few decorative random stitches in each centre to give it a little texture. With a tapestry needle and a little brown yarn, make a couple of straight stitches vertically under the circles to represent the tree trunks.

Stitch sequins, beads and pretty buttons on the castle for decoration. You can make the castle as elaborately decorated and colourful as you like.

FLAGS

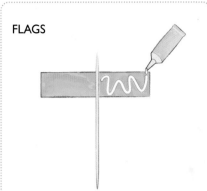

Take the orange and bright pink felt strips and place your cocktail stick in the centre, put a little glue on one side of the felt.

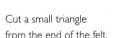

Fold the two sides of felt together over the cocktail stick to make a small flag shape. Set aside to dry.

Cut a small triangle from the end of the felt.

Push the cocktail stick into the top of the turret. You can add another drop of glue if you wish to keep it in place.

Put your bright pink flag into the top of the tall turret and the orange flag into the shorter turret in the centre.

Skill level: ★★★

Size

24 × 6.5 × 17cm (9½ × 2½ × 6¾in)

You will need

- DK (light worsted) yarn:
  50g (1¾oz) of white (A)
  30g (1oz) each of green (B) and dark
  brown (C)
  20g (¾oz) each of red (D), pink (E)
  and lime green (F)
- 3mm (US D/3) crochet hook
- Tapestry needle
- White sewing thread
- Sewing needle
- Toy stuffing
- Cardboard box without lid measuring
  23 × 7.5 × 4cm (9 × 3 × 1½in), such as
  the base from a cereal box cut to fit
- 4 bamboo skewers 15cm (6in) long –
  or lengths of medium gauge wire
- 38cm (15in) square of lace or netting
- 4 wooden beads, 1cm (⅜in) diameter
- Parcel tape (or other strong sticky
  tape)
- PVA glue

Abbreviations

ch	chain
ch sp	chain space
dc	double crochet
htr	half treble
rep	repeat
ss	slip stitch
t-ch	turning chain
tr	treble
yrh	yarn round hook

Special abbreviations

Qtr (quadruple treble) – yrh 4 times,
insert hook in next st, yrh, pull up a loop
(6 loops on hook), *yrh, draw yarn
through 2 loops; rep from * until 1 loop
remains on hook (1qtr made).
3ch picot – 3ch, ss in 3rd ch from hook.
5ch picot – 5ch, ss in 5th ch from hook.

THE ROYAL BED

All enchanted princesses need a comfortable bed, especially if they are going to spend a hundred years dozing and dreaming! Using scraps of yarn, fabrics and recycled boxes with other humble household materials, I have made a royal bed fit for even the sleepiest princess!

VALANCE

Sides:

(make 2)

Row 1: Using yarn B, 48ch, 1tr in 4th ch from hook, 1tr in each ch across, turn. (45 sts)
Rows 2–3: 3ch (counts as 1tr now and throughout), tr across, turn. (45 sts)
Fasten off.

Ends:

(make 2)

Row 1: Using B, 17ch, 1tr in 4th ch from hook, tr across, turn. (14 sts)
Rows 2–3: 3ch, tr across, turn.
Fasten off.
Using tails, sew sides and ends together to make one long piece.

Edging:

Work along the bottom of the valance as follows:
Row 1: Join yarn D to any corner st, 1ch, dc in same st, [3ch, miss 1 st, dc in next st] 58 times, 3ch, ss to first dc to join. (59 ch sps)

Row 2: Ss into first ch sp, 1ch, 5dc in each ch sp around, ss in first dc to join
Fasten off.

BEDCOVER

Row 1: Using yarn A, 17ch, 1tr in 4th ch from hook, tr across, turn. (14 sts)
Rows 2–21: 3ch, tr across, turn. (14 sts)
Do not fasten off.

Edging:

Work around all four sides of rectangle as follows:
Ch6, 2qtr in base of ch, 12qtr, 3qtr in last st, work 2qtr in each row-end along the side of rectangle, 3qtr in corner, 1qtr in each ch of the base ch, 3qtr in corner, 2qtr in each row-end along the side of rectangle, ss in 6th ch of t-ch to join. (120 sts)

Frill:

*2ch, [3ch picot, 5ch picot, 3ch picot], miss 1 st, 2ch, ss in next st, ss in next st, 3ch, ss in next st; rep from * 24 times.
Fasten off.

CANOPY FRILL

Row 1: Using yarn A, 112ch, 1htr in 3rd ch from hook, *1ch, miss 1 ch, 1htr in next ch; rep from * across. (55 sts)

Row 2: Work as Bedcover frill, counting the ch sps as sts. (22 repeats)

Fasten off.

PILLOW

Row 1: Using yarn A, 13ch, 1dc in 2nd ch from hook, dc across, turn. (12 sts)

Rows 2–16: 1ch, dc across, turn.

Fasten off.

Fold piece in half at Row 8, stitch both sides together, fill the pillow with a little toy stuffing and sew top edges closed.

Weave in ends.

FLOWERS AND LEAVES

Small roses:

(make 5)

Row 1: Using yarn E, 17ch, ss in 2nd ch from hook, [3ch, 1tr in next ch, ss into next ch] 5 times.

Fasten off.

Using the tail, make a row of running stitches through the base ch and draw up into a spiral, stitch through the centre to make the rosette shape and secure in place.

Weave in ends.

Large rose:

Row 1: Using yarn E, 31ch, ss in 2nd ch from hook, [3ch, 1tr in next ch, 2tr in next ch, 1tr in next ch, ss in next ch] 6 times.

Fasten off yarn and rep finishing as for smaller rose.

Leaves:

(make 7)

First side: Using yarn F, 6ch, *ss in 2nd ch from hook, 1dc in next ch, 3tr in next ch, 1dc in each of next 2 chs, ss in last ch; 1ch, rep from * along other side of base chain.

Fasten off.

MAKING THE BED

Before assembling, block each piece gently. Place the valance over the box and stitch in place. Place the bedcover on top of the bed with the frill hanging over the sides. Stitch or glue in place.

Posts:

Carefully push each bamboo post through the bed cover and box at each corner. To keep the posts in place, attach with some sticky tape to the underside of the box. Using yarn C, wrap each post from bottom to top, stitching through the wrappings occasionally to hold in place. When each post is fully covered, fasten off.

Canopy:

Place the square of net over the posts and centre, then push the net down over the ends of the posts. On one long side cut an opening to make two drapes on the front of the bed. Most net or factory made lace will not fray much, but for a really neat finish you can hem the edges.

To keep the canopy in place, put a little PVA glue onto the end of each post, push a wooden bead onto it and press down gently to keep the bead stuck down securely.

With sewing thread and needle, make a few stitches to hold the 2 drapes to the posts.

FINISHING

Attach the canopy frill around each side of canopy, stitching it to each post to keep in place.

Roses and leaves:

Stitch the leaves to the back of the roses. It looks better to vary the amount of leaves so that one rose may have one leaf attached, while another rose may have two leaves.

Stitch a small rose and leaf to each post at the front of the bed, stitch a rose in the centre front.

Stitch a small rose to each side of bottom of posts keeping the drapes in place.

Stitch the larger rose on one side next to the small rose.

Chapter 2

Fairytale Townsfolk

Where do the fabulous characters in our beloved tales reside? Why in Fairy Town of course, alongside our own hectic, noisy world but out of sight most of the time. Sometimes, though, these two worlds collide and we get to live our own magical adventure. Perhaps, like Little Jack, we climb a magical beanstalk and encounter a lumbering giant, or we catch a brief glimpse of a couple of friendly elves with superb shoe-making skills – or maybe we experience a chance encounter with irritable Rumpelstiltskin in a forest clearing.

Size

Approx 13.5cm (5¼in) tall

You will need

- DK (light worsted) yarn:
  20g (¾oz) of pale green (B)
  Small quantities of rust or orange (A),
  olive green (C), light brown (D), dark
  green (E), yellow green (F) and black
- 3mm (US D/3) crochet hook
- Removable stitch marker
- Tapestry needle
- Toy stuffing
- Embroidery thread or 2ply yarn in co-
  ordinating colours
- Medium gauge wire – one 15cm (6in)
  length; one 24cm (9½in) length
- Small pliers

Abbreviations

blo	back loop only
ch	chain
cont	continue
dc	double crochet
dc2tog	double crochet two sts together
htr	half treble
LH	left hand
pm	place marker
rem	remaining
rep	repeat
RS	right side
ss	slip stitch
st(s)	stitch(es)
t-ch	turning chain
tr	treble
WS	wrong side

The Elves and the Shoemaker

Ginger and Oakie are two friendly elves who help the kindly shoemaker. Ginger has a beard and red hair, while Oakie sports an acorn cap and acorn leaf pants. These little elfin characters are really easy to make, if a little bit fiddly. They have wire-wrapped arms and legs, which makes them unsuitable as toys for small children but you could always substitute cotton cord to make a softer elf.

GINGER

Head:

Round 1: Using yarn B, 3ch, 12tr in 2nd ch from hook, ss in first tr to join, pm. (12 sts)
Round 2: 1ch, dc around. (12 sts)
Round 3: [1dc, 2dc in next st] 6 times. (18 sts)
Rounds 4–5: Rep Round 2. (18 sts)
Round 6: 1ch, [dc2tog] 9 times. (9 sts)
Fill head with toy stuffing.

Neck and body:

Round 7: 1ch, [dc2tog] 4 times, 1dc. (5 sts)
Round 8: 1ch, [2dc in next st, 1dc] twice, 2dc in last st, ss in first dc to join. (8 sts)
Round 9: 1ch, [2dc into next st, 1dc] 4 times. (12 sts)
Round 10: 1ch, [2dc, 2dc in next st, 3dc] twice, ss in first dc to join. (14 sts)
Rounds 11–14: 1ch, dc around. (14 sts)
Fasten off yarn B.
Move st marker to centre back of Round 14.
Round 15: Join yarn C at st marker, dc around. (14 sts)
Round 16: 3ch (counts as 1tr now and throughout), 2tr in base of ch (centre back) miss 1 st, 4dc, 3tr in next st, miss 1 st, 4dc, miss last st, ss in 3rd ch of t-ch to join. (15 sts)

Fasten off yarn C.
Fill body with toy stuffing.

HAIR

Base ring: Using yarn A, 4ch (counts as 1tr, 1ch), 11tr in 3rd ch from hook, ss in top of t-ch to join. (12 sts)
Round 1: 2ch (counts as 1htr now and throughout), 1htr, 7tr, 1htr. (9 sts)
Leave the rem 2 sts unworked.
Fasten off.

BEARD

Row 1: Using yarn A, 11ch and, starting in 2nd ch from hook, work as follows: 3dc, 3ch, 1htr in next ch, 2tr, 1htr, 3dc.
Fasten off.

OAKIE
Head:

Base ring: Using yarn D, ch4 (counts as 1tr, 1ch), 13tr in 4th ch from hook, ss in top of t-ch to join, pm. (14 sts)
Round 1: 3ch, tr around.
Rounds 2–5: 1ch, dc around.
Round 6: 1ch, [dc2tog] 7 times, ss in first dc to join. (7 sts)
Fill head with toy stuffing.

Neck and body:

Round 7: 1ch, [1dc, dc2tog] twice, 1dc. (5 sts)
Round 8: 1ch, 2dc in each st around. (10 sts)
Round 9: 1ch, 2dc in first st, 5dc, 2dc in next st, dc to end of round. (12 sts)
Round 10: 1ch, [2dc, 2dc in next st, 3dc] twice. (14 sts)
Rounds 11–14: 1ch, dc around.
Fasten off yarn B.
Round 15: Join yarn E in blo at st marker, dc(blo) around, ss to first dc to join. (14 sts)

Oak leaf skirt:

Round 16: *5ch, ss back in each ch, ss in next 3 sts; rep from * 3 more times, 5ch, ss back in each ch, ss in next 3 sts. (5 fronds)
Fasten off yarn E.

Round 17: Join yarn F at the base of any 5ch frond, *[5ch, miss 1 ch, ss in next ch] 5 times, 2dc; rep from * 4 times.
Fill body with toy stuffing.
Weave in all ends neatly.

ACORN HAT

Base ring: Using yarn G, 5ch, join with ss in a ring, 1ch, 8dc in ring, ss in first ch to join. (8 sts)
Round 1: 1ch, 2dc in each st around, ss in first dc to join. (16 sts)
Rounds 2–3: 1ch, dc around, ss to first dc to join.
Turn to WS, ss(blo) to move yarn nearer to the centre, 9ch, ss into each ch from hook, making a cord.
Fasten off yarn G, weave in ends, then pull ch cord through centre of base ring to make a stalk.
Turn cap back to RS.

FINISHING

Attach beard and hair to Ginger in desired position using yarn tails.
Attach acorn hat to Oakie in desired position using yarn tail.
Put wire arms and legs through each body and wrap with yarn B (see page 125 for detailed instructions). When all exposed wire is covered with yarn and you are happy with position of limbs, stitch securely in place to torso. Stitch edge of Round 15 to wire legs. Weave in all ends except yarn A neatly.

Embroidery:

See pages 122–123 for embroidery stitches and page 124 for making a face. Using black yarn and darning needle, insert needle under hair to hide and draw through front of face, make two French knots to represent eyes. Use yarn B to make another French knot to represent a nose.

Oakie's pointed ears:

Using yarn B, insert hook into any surface st at side of head (two rounds below the acorn hat), yrh, pull up a loop, 3ch, 3tr in base of ch.
Fasten off. Rep for other ear. Weave in ends.
Bend arms and legs into position.

Tip

You can make the elves free standing or attach a loop to the top of the head to make a hanging decoration.

Skill level: ★★ / ★★★

Size

Chairs: 10cm (4in) tall
Table: 5cm (2in) tall

You will need

- DK (light worsted) yarn:
  Small amounts of red, gold,
  aqua and green
  10g (⅜oz) of white
  10g (⅜oz) of brown or dark green
- 3mm (US D/3) crochet hook
- Medium gauge wire – four 25cm
  (10in) lengths; two 20cm (8in) lengths;
  two 15cm (6in) lengths
- Toy stuffing
- 6.5cm (2½in) diameter jam jar lid or
  circle of card
- Tapestry needle
- Pair of pliers
- Wire cutters
- Glue suitable for metal and plastic

Abbreviations

beg	beginning
blo	back loop only
ch	chain
ch sp	chain space
dc	double crochet
rep	repeat
ss	slip stitch
st(s)	stitch(es)
t-ch	turning chain
tr	treble
WS	wrong side

ELF FURNITURE

All elves need some little chairs and tables to enjoy a cup of acorn tea and a plate of fairy bread, after a hard night of stitching leather boots and slippers. These wire pieces are trimmed with crocheted seats, cushions and table covers but there is scope for lots of customizing to make them as plain or fancy as you like.

These shy little creatures live alongside us in our homes and help with smaller household tasks – they prefer to remain unseen and usually work at night while we are fast asleep. They especially enjoy nibbling porridge and honey although Oakie, in particular, is partial to a little toast. Elves are easily offended and will leave the house if they feel that their hard work is not appreciated or if you try to pay them for their labour. Knowing this, the kindly shoemaker and his wife chose to reward them by not only providing them with warm, crocheted clothes but also by fashioning some delicate elf-sized furniture so that they can enjoy a midnight snack in comfort. The bright primary colours of the clothing and furniture could easily be substituted with soft greens and browns to give the elves some camouflage. Delicate beads, sequins or tiny fake flowers could be stitched to both clothing and furniture to give them true fairy glamour.

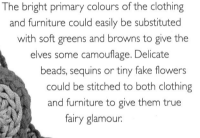

WIRE CHAIRS

The construction of the wire chairs (especially at the beginning) can be quite tricky. If the wire slips around too much, use a little sticky tape to hold it together. Once yarn is wrapped around the wire it will be covered over.

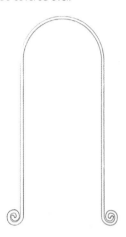

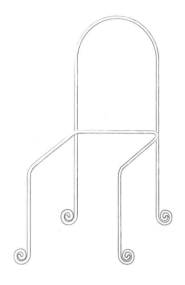

Bend the first 20cm (8in) length of wire into a deep upside down U shape for the back legs and chair back. Using the pliers curl the ends over into a neat rounded end to form the feet of the chair legs.

Repeat with the other 20cm (8in) length of wire. On this piece, halfway along the U shape, bend the wire at right angles to make the front legs and seat base.

Square off the rounded corners at the top of the U shape so the seat base will fit across the seat back.

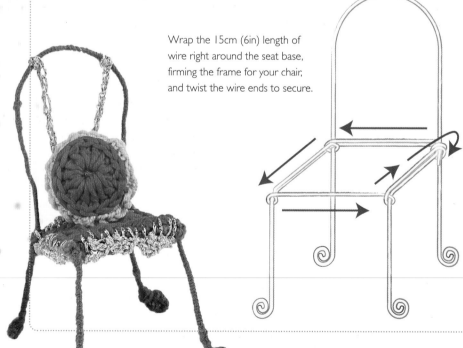

Wrap the 15cm (6in) length of wire right around the seat base, firming the frame for your chair, and twist the wire ends to secure.

Start wrapping dark green yarn along the wire frame as for wire arms and legs (see page 125). Continue until the chair frame is covered. Thread a tapestry needle with yarn and stitch and wrap through the joined wires forming the seat base until the chair feels stable. Make a few final stitches to secure the end and cut the yarn.

Tip

To make your chairs stronger, spray the crochet with a fabric stiffener or a spray starch.

CHAIR BACKS

Horizontal bar chairback:
With yarn of choice, 8ch.
Fasten off, leaving a long tail. Use tail to stitch chain across back of chair.

Vertical bar chairback:
Use gold yarn, 12ch, fasten off leaving a long tails. Use tail to attach vertically in a diagonal pattern on back of chair. Add more chains or experiment with different combinations to make a more fancy chair back if desired.

CROCHET SEAT
(make 2)
Using chosen colour, 4ch, ss in first ch to form a ring.
Round 1: 5ch (acts as 1tr, 2ch), [3tr in ring, 2ch] 3 times, 2tr in ring, ss in 3rd ch of t-ch to join. (4 groups of 3 tr)
Round 2: Ss into next ch sp, 3ch, [2tr, 2ch, 3tr] in same ch sp, *ch1, miss 3 tr, [3tr, 2ch, 3tr] in next corner ch sp; rep from * three times, 1ch, miss 3 sts, ss in 3rd ch of t-ch to join. (8 groups of 3 tr)
Fasten off. Use yarn tails to stitch crochet seat to the wire seat base.

Edgings:
Simple edge (shown in red): Attach yarn to any st, ss around. Fasten off.

Scallop frill (shown in gold): Attach yarn to any st, 1ch, dc around (capturing the wire frame within the st), ss to first dc to join. *5ch, miss 1 st, 1dc; rep from * around, ss in base of first 5ch to join. Fasten off.

CUSHIONS
(make 2)
Using first colour, 5ch, ss in first ch to form a ring.
Round 1: 3ch, 13tr in ring, ss in 3rd ch of t-ch to join. (14 sts)
Fasten off.
Make a second circle.
Hold the circles WS together, and (working

TABLE
Bend the two lengths of wire into deep U shapes as before. Using the pliers curl the ends over into a neat rounded end, forming feet that match the chairs. Wrap both wires with yarn as described on page 126. Place one U over the other and stitch the two shapes together to make a four-legged base for the table.

Using a strong glue suitable for metal and plastic, stick the top of the base in the middle of the underside of the jam jar lid. Set aside to dry.

When dry, using same colour yarn as wrapping, stitch around table legs using a darning needle, weaving around each leg and stitching through to make more secure.

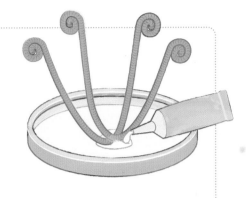

through both circles to crochet them together) join contrasting yarn to any tr. Work as follows (filling with toy stuffing before closing with the final sts):
Round 2: 1ch, [1dc, 1ch] 14 times, ss to first dc to join.
Fasten off yarn.
Rep for second cushion.

TABLECLOTH
Using white yarn, 2ch, 10dc in 2nd ch from hook, ss in first dc to join. (10 sts)
Round 1: 3ch, 1tr in base of ch, 2tr in each st to around, ss in 3rd ch of t-ch to join round. (20 sts)
Round 2: Rep Round 1. (40 sts)
Round 3: 3ch, 1tr in base of ch, [1tr, 2tr in next st] to last st, 1tr, ss in 3rd ch of t-ch to join. (60 sts)
Round 4: 1ch, dc(blo) around.

Scallop edging:
Round 5: [1dc, miss 1 st, 5tr in next st, miss 2 sts] 12 times, ss in first dc to join. (12 scallops)
Fasten off, weave in ends.
Stick the tablecloth to top and sides of table with a little glue (or sticky tape) and leave to dry.

"The poor shoemaker had only enough leather for one pair of shoes"

Skill level: ★★

Size

To fit elves

You will need

- DK (light worsted) yarn:
  Small quantities of red (A) and
  blue (B)
- 3mm (US D/3) crochet hook
- Removable stitch marker
- Tapestry needle
- Felt pompoms, 1cm (⅜in) diameter
- 3 buttons or beads, 1cm (⅜in)
  diameter
- Embroidery thread

Abbreviations

ch	chain
dc	double crochet
dc2tog	double crochet two sts together
pm	place marker
rep	repeat
ss	slip stitch
st(s)	stitch(es)
tr	treble
yrh	yarn round hook

ELF WEAR

The very latest in elfin attire, lovingly made by hand by kindly shoemaker's wives in cosy yarn to keep those industrious little elves warm on chilly nights. Ginger loves the bobble hat and tasselled scarf and pulls on the crocheted breeches immediately. Oakie eagerly slips on the bow tie sweater and boots.

BREECHES

Row 1: Using yarn A, 28ch, 1tr in 4th ch from hook and each ch to end, turn. (25 sts)
Round 2: 3ch (counts as 1tr now and throughout), tr across, turn. (25 sts)
Round 3: Insert hook through next st, miss 12 sts, insert hook through next st, miss 11 sts, insert hook through next st, yrh, draw yarn through all sts, leaving 1 loop on hook, creating 2 leg-holes.

Legs:

Work in rounds, making each leg one at a time, as follows:
Rounds 1–3: Dc around. (12 sts)
Round 4: [Dc2tog] 6 times. (6 sts)
Fasten off and weave in ends.
Rep Rounds 1–4 on the second leg.

Braces:

Ss in any slightly off-centre st at front of breeches, 14ch, ss in matching st at back of breeches.
Rep evenly on other side. Place on elf to check fit if required before fastening off.
Stitch a couple of tiny buttons or beads at front of breeches below braces.

BOBBLE HAT

Using yarn B, 2ch, 7dc in 2nd ch from hook, ss in first dc to join. (7 sts)
Round 1: 1ch, 2dc in each st around, ss in first dc to join. (14 sts)
Round 2: 1ch, 2dc in first st, 1dc, [2dc in next st, 3dc] three times, 1dc, ss in first dc to join. (18 sts)
Round 3: 1ch, dc around, ss in first dc to join.
Stitch a contrasting pompom to middle of hat (or attach with PVA glue if preferred).
Fasten off yarn and weave in ends.

SCARF

Using yarn B, 41ch, 1dc in 2nd ch from hook, 1dc in each ch to end, turn. (40 sts)
Row 1: 1ch, dc across. (40 sts)
Fasten off yarn, leaving 7.5cm (3in) end. Weave in all ends.
Make 2 tassels by winding a length of yarn A around two fingers several times, slip off and tie near one end. Cut through loops at other end. Using yarn tails, sew tassels to each end of scarf.

SWEATER FRONT

Row 1: Using yarn A, 13ch, 1dc in 2nd ch from hook, 1dc in each ch to end, turn. (12 sts)

Rows 2–5: 1ch, dc across.

Row 6: 1ch, dc2tog, 8dc, dc2tog. (10 sts)

Row 7: 1ch, dc2tog, 6dc, dc2tog. (8 sts)

Row 8: 1ch, [dc2tog] 4 times. (4 sts)

Row 9: Rep Row 2.

Fasten off. Weave in ends.

SWEATER BACK

(make 2)

Row 1: Using yarn A, 7ch, 1dc in 2nd ch from hook, 1dc in each ch across. (6 sts)

Rows 2–5: 1ch, dc across.

Row 6: 1ch, dc2tog, 4dc. (5 sts)

Row 7: 1ch, 3dc, dc2tog. (4 sts)

Row 8: 1ch, dc2tog, 2dc. (3 sts)

Row 9: 1ch, 2dc, fasten off (leaving 1 st unworked). (2 sts)

Button loop:

Make on straight edge of one Back only as follows: Using yarn A, 8ch, ss in same st as ch to make a loop.

Seam front and backs together at short straight edges. Leave shaped sections open for sleeves.

Sleeves:

Round 1: Join yarn A at shoulder, 1ch, pm, 12dc evenly around. (12 sts)

Round 2: 1ch, [dc2tog, 4dc] twice, ss in first dc to join. (10 sts)

Rounds 3–6: 1ch, dc around, ss in first dc to join.

Fasten off, weave in ends.

Rep for second sleeve.

Stitch small button to Back to match loop on other side.

Tip

Use up all your scraps of yarn in different shades to make a colourful wardrobe for the elves.

To make bow, join yarn B to any st in centre front, 15ch, fasten off and weave end into ch to secure.

Tie both ends together in a bow.

BOOTS

(make 2)

Round 1: Using yarn B, 2ch, 6dc in 2nd ch from hook, ss in first dc join, pm. (6 sts)

Rounds 2–4: Dc around.

Round 4: 3ch, 2tr, 4dc. (6 sts)

Round 5: 1dc, dc2tog, 3dc. (5 sts)

Rounds 6–9: Dc around.

Fasten off, weave in ends.

Stitch a contrast pompom or bead to end of each toe.

Skill level: ★★

Size

House: 4.5cm (1¾in) high
Beanstalk: 21.5cm (8½in) high (including base)

You will need

- DK (light worsted) yarn:
  30g (1oz) of olive green (A)
  10g (⅜oz) of medium green (B)
  10g (⅜oz) of light green (C)
  Small amounts of cream (D)
  and grey (E)
- 3mm (US D/3) crochet hook
- Tapestry needle
- Embroidery thread or 2ply yarn in
  pale green or blue
- Medium gauge wire – 30cm
  (12in) length
- Felt – two 10cm (4in) diameter circles
  in green or brown; offcuts in pink and
  black
- Toy stuffing
- Fabric stiffener (optional)
- Double-sided sticky tape (optional)

Abbreviations

blo	back loop only
ch	chain
ch sp	chain space
dc	double crochet
htr	half treble
tr	treble
rep	repeat
ss	slip stitch
st(s)	stitch(es)
t-ch	turning chain

Tip

It's a good idea to wrap a little double-sided sticky tape onto the wire before you start wrapping the yarn to help the yarn stay in place.

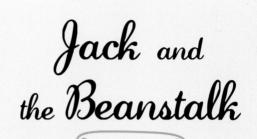

Jack and the Beanstalk

BEANSTALK AND COTTAGE

This cute little project seems fiddly to put together, but it is made using mostly double crochet. There is a lot of opportunity for you to customize the pattern if you wish. The scale of the tiny cottage gives the beanstalk a magical giant quality but you could just make the beanstalk if you like. It makes a fun scene setter for storytelling or could be used as an unusual pin cushion.

GRASS HILL

With yarn A, 5ch, ss in first ch to make a ring.

Round 1: 3ch (counts as 1tr now and throughout), 1tr in ring [3ch, 2tr in ring] 5 times, 3ch, ss in 3rd ch of t-ch to join. (6 tr groups)

Round 2: 3ch, 1tr, [3ch, miss ch sp, work 1tr in each tr of next tr group] 5 times, 3ch, ss in 3rd ch of t-ch to join. (6 tr groups)
Fasten off yarn A.

Round 3: Join yarn B to any ch sp. 1ch, [4dc in ch sp, 1ch] in each ch sp around, ss in first dc to join. (24 dc and 6 ch sps)
Fasten off yarn B.

Round 4: Join yarn A to any dc. 1ch, dc around (working 1dc in each ch sp), ss to first dc to join. (30 sts)
Fasten off yarn A.

Round 5: Join yarn C to any st. 1ch, 2dc each st around, ss in first dc to join. (60 sts)
Fasten off yarn C.

Round 6: Join yarn A to any st. 1ch, dc around, ss in first dc to join.

Round 7: 1ch, [1dc, dc2tog] 20 times. (40 sts)
Fasten off yarn A.
Weave in ends.
Place a felt circle on the underside of the crochet dome shape and neatly backstitch in place using a length of yarn.

BEANSTALK

Take the 30cm (12in) length of wire, push one end through the crochet and felt dome (making a small cut in the felt if required), bend a small loop at each end of wire, bend the loop into a right angle shape on the under side of the crochet/felt circle and stitch in place (using yarn A) to secure. Take the needle back through to the right side of crochet dome and start to tightly wrap the yarn around the wire. Continue to cover the wire in yarn until fully covered, stitch through the loop at the end of wire a few times to cover the loop and secure the yarn. Fasten off.

LEAVES

(make 2 small and 1 large)

Small:

Using yarn A, 8ch, ss into first ch from hook.

Work in each ch as follows:

1dc, 1htr, 1tr, 2tr in next ch, 1tr, 1htr, 1dc, 1ch. Rep pattern along other side of ch to make a leaf shape, ss in first ss to join.

Fasten off A.

Large:

Rep Small Leaf and work a second round as follows:

2ch, 3htr, 1tr, 3tr in next st, 1tr, 3htr, ss in pointed end, 3htr in same st, rep along other side of leaf shape, ss in 2nd ch to join.

Fasten off.

Attach the leaves in desired position onto the wrapped wire. Weave in ends to the backs of the leaves.

When you are happy with the amount of leaves, you can then bend the wire into a curling, organic shape.

"Where the magic beans had landed, a great beanstalk had grown"

JACK'S COTTAGE

Base:

Row 1: Using yarn D, 5ch, 1dc in 2nd ch from hook, 3dc, turn. (4 sts)

Rows 2–4: 1ch, dc across, turn.

Walls:

Work into the base as follows:

Round 1: 1ch, 4dc(blo) rotate base to work 4dc along the side, rotate base to work 5dc(blo) along base chain, rotate to work 4dc along side, ss in first dc to join. (16 sts)

Rounds 2–4: 1ch, dc around, ss to first dc to join. (16 sts)

Fasten off yarn D.

Roof:

Round 5: Join yarn E to same corner st, 1ch, dc around, ss to first dc to join. (16 sts)

Round 6: Rep Round 4.

Round 7: [Dc2tog] 8 times. (8 sts)

Use a little toy stuffing to fill your house shape. Fold last round in half, giving you two sides of 4 sts each, ss together. (4 sts)

Chimney:

Join yarn D to last st of roof, 1ch, 2dc.

Fasten off and weave in ends.

FINISHING

Cut two tiny squares of black felt and stitch or glue them in place to represent windows and a small rectangle of pink felt as a door.

Using a piece of pale green thread or 2ply yarn, neatly stitch a cross stitch over each window. Using the same thread attach the cottage onto to the hill at the side of the beanstalk.

Sew the dome to the other pre-cut circle of felt carefully, using backstitch or a blanket stitch, with sewing thread or 2ply yarn in a co-ordinating shade of green.

Leave a little space, insert the toy stuffing into dome shape, and stitch up the gap.

Skill level: ★★

Size

30cm (12in) tall

You will need

- DK (light worsted) yarn:
  20g (¾oz) of black (A)
  30g (1oz) each of flesh tone (B) and
  taupe/light brown (C)
  20g (¾oz) of white (F)
- Aran (worsted) yarn:
  30g (1oz) each of green (D)
  and grey (E)
- Garden twine/string – three 30cm
  (12in) lengths
- Toy stuffing
- 3mm (US D/3) crochet hook
- 5mm (US H/8) crochet hook
- Removable stitch marker
- Tapestry needle
- Black embroidery thread or 2ply yarn

Abbreviations

ch	chain
dc	double crochet
dc2tog	double crochet two sts together
flo	front loop only
htr	half treble
rem	remain(ing)
ss	slip stitch
st(s)	stitch(es)
t-ch	turning chain
tr	treble

GIANT

This friendly looking fellow towers over the other figures in this book – when stood next to Little Jack (see page 64), you can see how big he is! He is made in simple double and treble crochet and worked in the round from his head down. The boots or buskins are made separately and then stitched on at the end.

HEAD

Base ring: Using yarn B and 3 mm (US D/3 hook), 5ch, ss in 5th ch from hook to join.

Round 1: 3ch (counts as 1tr now and throughout), 11tr into ring, ss in 3rd ch of t-ch to join. (12 sts)

Round 2: 3ch, 1tr in base of ch, 2tr in each st around, ss in 3rd ch of t-ch to join. (24 sts)

Round 3: 3ch, [2tr into next st, 1tr into next st] 11 times, 2tr in last st, ss in 3rd ch of t-ch to join. (36 sts)

Place st marker and, moving the st marker at the end of each round, work in spirals as follows:

Rounds 4–10: Dc around. (36 sts)

Stubble:

For the next 5 rounds you will be changing colour mid-round, so you will need to loosely weave the yarn not being worked across the back loops of the sts to ensure that the sections do not pucker up. To do this, simply lay the yarn not in use over working yarn at back of work before you make your next st.

Rounds 11–12: Using yarn C, 16dc, change to yarn B, 20dc. (36 sts)

Round 13: Using yarn C, [dc2tog] 8 times (8 sts of C rem), change to yarn B, [dc2tog] 10 times (10 sts of B rem). (18 sts)

Round 14: Using yarn C, 8dc, change to yarn B, 10dc. (18 sts)

"Fee fi fo fum, I smell the blood of an Englishman"

Round 15: Using yarn C, dc2tog, 1dc into next 6 sts (7 sts of C rem), change to yarn B, dc2tog, 1dc into each of next 8 sts (9 sts of B rem), ss in first dc to join round. (16 sts)

Fasten off both yarns, leaving 7.5cm (3in) tails. Fill head with toy stuffing.

You will work the giant's body with a 5mm (US H/8) hook and aran weight yarn. From now on you will be working in the round using the appropriate number of ch at beg and a ss to join each round at end.

Neck:

Round 16: Switch to 5mm (US H/8) hook and yarn D. 1ch, dc around, ss into first dc to join. (16 sts)

Shoulders:

Round 17: 3ch, 1tr in base of ch, 2tr in each st around, ss in 3rd ch of t-ch to join. (32 sts)

Round 18: 3ch, tr around, ss in 3rd ch of t-ch to join. (32 sts)

Armholes and tunic:

Round 19: 3ch, 5tr, leave next 6 sts unworked, 10tr, leave next 6 sts unworked, 5tr, ss in 3rd ch of t-ch to join.

This makes two armholes of 6 sts each and a central trunk of 20 sts.

Continue to work in centre 20 sts only as follows:

Round 20: 3ch, [2tr in next st, 9tr] twice, 1tr, ss in 3rd ch of t-ch to join. (22 sts)

Round 21: 3ch, [2tr in next st, 1tr] 10 times, 2tr in last st, ss in 3rd ch of t-ch to join. (33 sts)

Round 22: 3ch, tr around, ss in 3rd ch of t-ch to join. (33 sts)

Fasten off yarn D, leaving a 7.5cm (3in) tail. Fill body with toy stuffing.

Breeches:

Round 23: Change to yarn E and attach to flo (WS) of tunic. 1ch, dc(flo) around, ss in first dc to join round. (33 sts)

Rounds 24–25: 1ch, dc around, ss in first dc to join.

Leg holes:

Set up round: Insert hook in next st, miss next 16 sts, insert hook into next st, yrh, draw yarn through both sts, leaving 1 loop on hook, miss next 16 sts, ss in first st. making two leg-holes of 16 sts each. Work into each leg-hole (in spirals) as follows:

Leg rounds 1–6: Place st marker. Dc around, moving the marker at the end of each round. (16 sts)

Leg round 7: [Dc2tog] 8 times. (8 sts)

Fasten off yarn E, leaving a 7.5cm (3in) tail. Attach yarn and repeat for second leg. Fill legs with toy stuffing.

Arms:

Using a 3mm (US D/3) hook and yarn F, rejoin yarn at armpit. Place st marker and work in spirals as follows:

Round 1: 2dc in join of armpit, [2dc in next st, 1dc] twice, 2dc in last st. (10 sts)

Rounds 2–7: Dc around. (10 sts)

Round 8: [Dc2tog] 5 times. (5 sts)

Round 9: Dc around, ss in first dc to join. (5 sts)

Fasten off yarn F, leaving a 7.5cm (3in) tail. Fill arms with toy stuffing.

Hands:

Round 10: Attach yarn B to any st at wrist, place st marker, dc around. (5 sts)

Round 11: 2dc in each st around. (10 sts)

Round 12: [2dc in next st, 1dc] 4 times, 2dc. (14 sts)

Fill hands with toy stuffing.

Thumbs:

Fold hand in half with 7 sts facing you and 7 sts facing the back.

Round 13: Insert hook into both first st facing you and the st directly behind it, and ss tog. Rep for next 3 sts, leaving the 4 front and 4 back sts. (8 sts in total)

Rounds 14–16: Working into these 8 sts only, dc around. (8 sts)

Fill finger section with toy stuffing.

Round 17: [Dc2tog] 4 times. (4 sts)

Fasten off yarn B and use the tail to stitch the finger section closed and weave in the end.

Rep for other arm.

BUSKINS (BOOTS)

(make 2)

Base ring: Using yarn C and 3mm (US D/3) hook, 2ch, 6dc in second ch from hook, ss in first dc to join. (6 sts)

Round 1: 3ch, 1tr in base of ch, 2tr in each st a round, ss in 3rd ch of t-ch to join. (12 sts)

Place st marker and work in spirals as follows:

Round 2: [1dc, 2dc in next st] 6 times. (18 sts)

Rounds 3–7: 1dc around.

Heel:

Round 8: 3ch, 9tr, leave rem 9 sts unworked, turn and work heel shaping as follows:

Row 9: 3ch, 9tr, turn. (9 sts)

Round 10: 2ch (counts as 1htr), 7tr, 1htr, dc in rem 9 sts of Round 8 to st marker. (18 sts)

Round 11: Dc around. (18 sts)

Round 12: [2dc in next st, 2dc] 6 times. (24 sts)

Rounds 13–18: Dc around, ss in first dc to join at end of last round.

Fasten off yarn C, leaving a 7.5cm (3in) tail.

Fill each boot with stuffing.

Hair:

Base ring: With yarn A and a 3mm (US D/3) hook, 5ch, ss in 5th ch from hook to join.

Round 1: 3ch, 11tr in ring, ss in 3rd ch of t-ch to join. (12 sts)

Round 2: 3ch, 1tr in base of ch, 2tr in each st around, ss in 3rd ch of t-ch to join. (24 sts)

Round 3: 3ch, [2tr in next st, 1tr] 11 times, 2tr in last st, ss in 3rd ch of t-ch to join. (36 sts)

Round 4: 3ch, 27tr, turn and (leaving rem 9 sts unworked) work in rows as follows:

Row 5: Ss in next 4 sts, 1tr into each of next 20 sts, turn (leaving rem 4 sts unworked). (20 sts)

Row 6: 3ch, 19tr, turn (leaving rem 4 sts unworked). (20 sts)

Row 7: Ss in next 4 sts, 3ch, 12tr (leaving 4 sts unworked). (16 sts)

Fasten off yarn A, leaving a 20cm (8in) tail.

Beard:

Using a 3mm (US D/3) hook and yarn A, reattach yarn to the edge of hair at Hair Round 4. Work 6 surface crochet dc down the side of the face following the curve of the head to chin, surface crochet 6dc across chin and 6dc up the other side of the face ss to Hair Round 4 to join. Fasten off, leaving a 7.5cm (3in) tail.

Re-attach yarn A at one side of 6 dc sts across chin, 2ch (counts as 1htr), 4tr, 1htr into last st. Fasten off yarn A. Weave in all ends to beard.

Bulbous nose:

Base ring: With 3mm (US D/3) hook and yarn B, 2ch, 6dc in 2nd ch from hook, ss in first dc to join. (6 sts)

Rounds 1–4: Dc around.

Round 5: [1dc, miss next st] 3 times. (3 sts)

Fasten off yarn B, use tapestry needle to draw tail through sts and tighten, leaving a 7.5cm (3in) tail.

FINISHING

Using tapestry needle and yarn A, stitch hair to head.

Using yarn B, stitch nose to face.

Using yarn C, stitch the boots in place on the legs. Stitch through boot to heel to shape foot into a standing position.

Tie a length of twine around each boot and cross over at front, tying at side in a bow.

Tie other piece of twine loosely around the waist to make a belt, secure with a slip knot.

Embroidery:

See pages 122–123 for embroidery stitches, and page 124 for making a face. Using yarn A, make two large French knot eyes.

With black embroidery thread, make eyebrows with two long stitches, slightly pointing downwards in the centre. For the mouth, make three straight stitches in a horseshoe shape.

Skill level: ★★

Size

12.5cm (5in) tall

You will need

- DK (light worsted) yarn:
  10g (⅜oz) each of dark brown (A)
  and flesh tone (B)
  20g (¾oz) each of bright green (C)
  and light brown (D)
  10g (⅜oz) of black (E)
- 3mm (US D/3) crochet hook
- Removable stitch marker
- Tapestry needle
- Toy stuffing
- Medium gauge wire – one 22cm
  (8¾in) length; one 12cm (4¾in) length
- Small pliers
- 1 x 7.5cm (⅜ x 3in) strip of
  brown felt
- Small amount of black sewing thread
- Sewing needle
- One small button

Abbreviations

ch	chain
cont	continue
dc	double crochet
dc2tog	double crochet two sts together
rem	remaining
rep	repeat
ss	slip stitch
st(s)	stitch(es)
t-ch	turning chain
tr	treble

LITTLE JACK

Little Jack is made in a very similar way to the elves with a yarn wrapped wire frame and a head and body worked in double crochet. He is free standing and is leaning back, looking at the Giant in wonder! Due to the wire used in the construction, Jack is not suitable for young children.

JACK

Head:

Base ring: Using yarn B, 2ch, 8dc in 2nd ch from hook, ss in first dc to join. (8 sts)
Place st marker and work in spirals, moving the st marker each round as follows:
Round 1: 2dc in each st around. (16 sts)
Rounds 2–6: Dc around. (16 sts)
Fill head with toy stuffing.
Round 7: [Dc2tog] 8 times. (8 sts)
Fasten off yarn B and weave in end.

Body:

Rounds 8–9: Change to yarn C. Dc around. (8 sts)
Round 10: [2dc in next st, 3dc] twice. (10 sts)
Round 11: [2dc in next st, 4dc] twice. (12 sts)
Round 12: [1dc, 2dc in next st] around. (18 sts)
Rounds 13–14: Dc around. (18 sts)
Fasten off yarn C, leaving a 7.5cm (3in) tail.
Do not put stuffing into body at this point as you will be putting wire and stuffing into body later on.

BREECHES

Base ring: Using yarn D, 5ch, ss in 5th ch from hook to join.
Round 1: 1ch, 9dc in ring, ss in first dc to join. (9 sts)
Round 2: 3ch (counts as 1tr now and throughout), 1 tr in base of ch, 2tr in each st around, ss in 3rd ch of t-ch to join. (18 sts)
Fasten off yarn D, leaving a 10cm (4in) tail.

HAIR

Base ring: Using yarn A, 2ch, 8dc in 2nd ch from hook, ss in first dc to join. (8 sts)
Round 1: Place st marker and cont in a spiral. 2dc in each st around. (16 sts)
Round 2: Dc around. (16 sts)
Round 3: 3ch, 10tr, leaving rem 6 sts unworked. Fasten off yarn A, leaving a 7.5cm (3in) tail.

FINISHING

Stitch hair to head using yarn A.

Arms:

Insert shorter 12cm (4¾in) wire through Jack's body at Round 9 and follow detailed instructions on page 125, using yarn B to wrap the hands and yarn C to wrap the arms to the shoulders.

Legs and feet:

For the legs, fold the 22cm (8¾in) wire length as described in step 4 on page 125. Insert inside Jack's head and body and through the breeches as described in step 5. Fill body with toy stuffing and stitch breeches to rest of the body at Round 14, using tail of yarn D.
Stand the figure up and bend the legs and feet into a standing position.
Using a length of yarn D, wrap the yarn around each wire leg to just above the loop foot until fully covered and cont to build layers of yarn D to make legs look thicker. Use yarn E to wrap round each foot and ankle in turn to look like black ankle boots.
Fasten off all yarn and trim closely when finished.

Embroidery:

As Jack is rather small I have just given him two small black French knot eyes. See page 122 for instructions.

Belt:

Wrap the strip of brown felt around Jack's waist and sew in place with black thread and sewing needle. Stitch a small button to the centre of belt as a buckle.

You can now bend Jack's body, arms and legs into your chosen position. I have bent his head back slightly so that he is looking up at the giant a little nervously!

Size

16.5cm (6½in) tall (including hat)

You will need

- DK (light worsted) yarn:
  10g (⅜oz) each of lime green (A),
  orange (B) and white (D)
  20g (¾oz) each of flesh tone (C), red
  (E) and olive green (F)
  Small amount of dark brown (G)
- 3mm (US D/3) crochet hook
- Removable stitch marker
- Tapestry needle
- Toy stuffing
- Medium gauge wire – one 12.5cm
  (5in) length; one 22cm (8¾in) length
- Embroidery thread or 2ply yarn in
  black and red
- 5 gold beads
- Metal button, 1.5cm (⅝in) diameter
- Small green feather
- Green and red sewing thread
- Sewing needle

Abbreviations

ch	chain
dc	double crochet
dc2tog	double crochet two sts together
pm	place marker
rep	repeat
ss	slip stitch
st(s)	stitch(es)
t-ch	turning chain
tr	treble
yrh	yarn round hook

Rumpelstiltskin

Rumpelstiltskin is dressed as a rather stylish Tudor gentleman of diminished stature and an irritable nature. He has a ginger moustache with bandy legs in stripy tights and he sports a feather in his hat. His body is wired so that he can be moved around and placed in different positions. He is made mostly using double crochet worked in spirals. His hat and hair are made separately and stitched on at the end.

HEAD AND BODY

Work from top of head down in a spiral.
Base ring: Using yarn C, 2ch, 10dc in 2nd ch from hook, ss in first dc to join. (10 sts)
Round 1: Pm, 2dc in each st around. (20 sts)
Rounds 2–8: Dc around.
Round 9: Dc2tog around. (10 sts)

Chin:

Round 10: 1dc, 3tr cluster in next st, dc. This creates a nobbly chin without increasing the stitch count. (10 sts)
Round 11: Dc around. (10 sts)
Fill head with toy stuffing.
Fasten off yarn C.

Neck:

Round 12: Join yarn E at st marker, dc around. (10 sts)
Round 13: 2dc in each st around. (20 sts)
Round 14: [2dc in next st, 4dc] 4 times. (24 sts)

Armholes:

Round 16: 4dc, miss 4 sts, 8dc, miss 4 sts, 4dc. This creates two armholes of 4 sts each and a body of 16 sts.
You will now work around the central 16 sts to make the body.

Body:

Rounds 17–19: Pm, dc around. (16 sts)

Peplum of jacket:

Worked in rounds.
Round 20: 3ch (counts as 1tr now and throughout), 1tr in base of ch, 2tr in each st around, ss to 3rd ch of t-ch to join. (32 sts)
Round 21: Rep Round 20. (64 sts)
Fasten off yarn E.
Fill body with toy stuffing.

Sleeves:

Sleeve round 1: Join yarn E at armpit, pm, 2dc in join, 1dc in next free st of armhole, 2dc in next free st of armhole, 1dc in last st. (6 sts)
Sleeve rounds 2–4: Dc around. (6 sts)
Sleeve round 5: [1dc, dc2tog] twice. (4 sts)
Sleeve rounds 6–8: 4dc, ss in first dc to join. (4 sts)
Fasten off yarn E.
Rep for second sleeve.

Special abbreviation

3tr cluster – *yrh, insert hook in the required stitch, yrh again and draw a loop through. Yrh, draw through 2 of the loops, leaving 2 loops on hook; rep from * twice more ending with 4 loops on hook, yrh and draw through all the loops on the hook to complete cluster.

"Rumpelstiltskin
is my name"

ARMS

Use the 12.5cm (5in) wire to make the arms as described on page 125. Use yarn C to wrap hands and arms.

RUFF

Base chain: Using yarn D, 18ch.
Row 1: 1tr in 4th ch from hook, 2tr in each ch to end. (30 sts)
Fasten off yarn D.

BREECHES

Worked in rows.
Base chain: Using yarn F, 17ch.
Row 1: 1dc in 2nd ch from hook, 1dc in each ch to end. (16 sts)
Row 2: 3ch, 1tr in base of ch, [1tr, 2tr in next st] 7 times, 1tr. (24 sts)
Row 3: 3ch, 2tr in next st, 22tr. (25 sts)

Legs:

Insert hook in 13th and 25th sts of Row 3, ss together creating two leg-holes of 12 sts each. Work in a spiral around each leg-hole separately as follows:
Round 4: Pm, dc around. (12 sts)
Round 5: Dc2tog around. (6 sts)
Fasten off yarn F.
Rejoin yarn F to second leg, rep Rounds 4–5 and fasten off.
Put a little stuffing into breeches.

LEGS

Make wire legs with the 22cm (8¾in) wire as described in step 4 on page 125, push through leg-holes of Breeches. Stitch the ends of leg-holes tightly around wires, using yarn F.

Stitch the back seam of breeches together and fill breeches with toy stuffing.

Stitch breeches to Round 19 (16 sts) inside the body and under the peplum. Wrap yarn D round wire leg and down to foot loop, stitching through yarn every so often to keep it in place. Continue to wrap and stitch until fully covered in yarn and resembling a leg shape. Change to yarn E and stitch through the wrapped yarn. Wrap a couple of times round leg in a stripe, stitching into wraps to secure. Rep stripe at regular intervals down to ankle area. Trim ends closely.

Boots:

With yarn G, wrap yarn around ankle and foot loop until fully covered. Fasten off neatly.

Rep for the second leg.

Bend feet upwards at a right angle until figure can stand up.

HAT

Worked from top of hat down.

Base ring: Using yarn A, 2ch, 6dc in second ch from hook, ss in first dc to join. (6 sts)

Rounds 1–3: Pm, dc around. (6 sts)

Round 4: [2dc in next st, 1dc] 3 times. (9 sts)

Round 5: 1dc, [2dc in next st, 1dc] 4 times. (13 sts)

Round 6: 1dc, [2dc in next st, 1dc] 6 times. (19 sts)

Round 7: Dc around. (19 sts)

Brim:

Round 8: 3ch, 1tr in base of ch, 2tr in each st around, ss in 3rd ch of t-ch to join round. (38 sts) Fasten off yarn A.

HAIR

Base chain: Using yarn B, 18ch.

Row 1: 3ch, 1tr in 4th ch from hook, 1tr in each ch to end. (15 sts)

Row 2: 3ch, tr across.

Fasten off yarn B, leaving a long tail.

FINISHING

Using the yarn tails, stitch the hat to the top of head; the hair around back of head under hat; the ruff around neck.

Using green sewing thread and sewing needle, sew the green feather to the side of the hat and stitch a decorative gold button on top as a brooch.

With red sewing thread, stitch 5 small gold buttons down the front of the jacket.

Embroidery:

For embroidery stitches see pages 122–123 and page 124 for making faces. Using yarn G, make two French knots for eyes.

Using yarn C, make one large French knot for nose, wrap yarn around knot 5 times and then stitch back through to make the nose bigger.

Using yarn B, stitch a curly line under his nose as a moustache.

Using a little red embroidery thread, make 3 small stitches to create a mouth.

Chapter 3

Tales from the Forest

My favourite tales have an element of darkness and danger that often stems from shadowy, enchanted forests. Strange magical creatures prowl through aged trees following unsuspecting travellers, watching until they leave the safety of the path. This forest is home to a wily gentleman wolf and a wicked witch who lives in a gingerbread cottage, but three clever children are more than a match for both villains, with a little assistance from a brave woodcutter. Amid the trees, in a sun-dappled clearing, a beautiful maiden with the longest hair awaits rescue by her handsome prince. The prince is a little busy, as I could not resist giving him a scary dragon to vanquish first!

Skill level: ★★

Size

Gretel – 10cm (4in) tall
Hansel – 11.5cm (4½in) tall

You will need

Gretel:
- DK (light worsted) yarn:
  Oddments of yellow (A), flesh tone or peach (B) and silver-green (F)
  10g (⅜oz) each of red (C) and pink (D)
- Scraps of coloured felt in greens and pinks
- 2.5cm (1in) square of cream felt
- Heart shape button

Hansel:
- DK (light worsted) yarn:
  10g (⅜oz) of brown (A), yellow (C), green (D) and red (E)
  Oddments of flesh tone or peach (B) and silver-green (F)

Both:
- 3mm (US D/3) crochet hook
- Removable stitch marker
- Toy stuffing
- Tapestry needle
- Embroidery thread or 2ply yarn in bright colours

Abbreviations

blo	back loop only
ch	chain
cont	continue
dc	double crochet
dc2tog	double crochet two sts together
dtr	double treble
htr	half treble
pm	place marker
ss	slip stitch
st(s)	stitch(es)
tr	treble
rep	repeat
rem	remaining
yrh	yarn round hook

Hansel and Gretel are brother and sister; they are quick to make and can be customized to your own wishes. I have made free standing figures but you could easily make cute egg cosies or finger puppets by omitting the skirt base and stitching a simple lining inside – if so, work Hansel's bottom half as for Gretel.

GRETEL

Head:

Using yarn B, 2ch, 6dc in 2nd ch, ss in first dc to join, pm.
Round 1: 2dc in each st around. (12 sts)
Rounds 2–5: Dc around. (12 sts)
Fill head with toy stuffing,
Round 6: [Dc2tog] 6 times. (6 sts)
Fasten off yarn B.
Fill head with toy stuffing.

Bodice:

Round 7: Join yarn C at st marker, dc(blo) around. (6 sts)
Round 8: 2dc in each st around, ss in first dc to join. (12 sts)
Rounds 9–10: Dc around.
Fasten off yarn C.

Skirt:

Round 11: Join yarn D at st marker, 3ch (counts as 1tr now and throughout), 1tr at base of ch, 2tr in each st to end. (24 sts)
Round 12: 3ch, tr around.
Round 13: Rep Round 9. (24 sts)
Fasten off yarn D.
Round 14: Join yarn F at st marker, 1ch, dc around, ss in first dc to join. (24 sts)
Round 15: [5ch, miss 2 sts, ss in next st] 12 times. (12 ch loops)
Fasten off yarn F.

Skirt base

Base ring: Using yarn C, 2ch, 6dc in 2nd ch, ss in first dc to join. (6 sts)
Round 1: 3ch, 1tr in base of ch, 2tr in each st around. (12 sts)
Round 2: 1ch, 2dc in each st around. (24 sts)
Fasten off yarn C, leaving a 15cm (6in) tail.

FINISHING

Fill bodice and skirt with toy stuffing. Use tail of Skirt Base to attach to inside skirt to contain the stuffing.

Hair:

Using yarn A, 2ch, 6dc in 2nd ch from hook, ss in first dc to join, pm.
Round 1: 2dc in each st around. (12 sts)
Round 2: [1htr, 1tr, 3dtr in next st, 1tr, 1htr, ss in next st] twice.
Fasten off A.

Plaits:

Cut 15cm (6in) length of yarn A, fold in half and put hook in fold, insert hook through end of dtr in Round 2, ss through dtr and 5ch using double thickness of A. Tie off and trim both ends of yarn to make a plait. Rep for other plait.
Use tail of yarn A to attach hair to head.

"Do come in, and stay with me"

Flower in hair:
Insert hook into surface of hair at one side, using yarn D, yrh and draw through loop, 5ch, ss in base of ch, 3ch, ss in base of ch. Fasten off and weave in ends.
Stitch a tiny green felt leaf next to flower.

Face:
For embroidery stitches see pages 122–123 and page 124 for making faces. Use French knots and black or brown yarn for eyes and peach for the nose. Make two tiny red stitches for a mouth and use cross stitch in pink to make 2 rosy cheeks.

Arms:
Follow the instructions on page 125; I have given Gretel long red sleeves but you can use any colour or sleeve length you like.

Apron:
Stitch cream piece of felt onto front of the skirt, shaping the bottom so it's rounded. Use a contrasting thread to stitch a tiny patch of felt onto skirt at side of the apron.

HANSEL
Head and Body:
Using yarn B, 2ch, 6dc in 2nd ch, ss in first dc to join, pm.
Round 1: 2dc in each st around. (12 sts)
Rounds 2–5: Dc around. (12 sts)
Fill head with toy stuffing.
Round 6: [Dc2tog] 6 times. (6 sts)
Fasten off yarn B.
Round 7: Join yarn C at st marker, dc around. (6 sts)
Round 8: 2dc in each st around. (12 sts)
Rounds 9–11: Dc around.
Fasten off yarn C.
Fill body with toy stuffing.

Knickerbockers:
Round 12: Join yarn D at st marker, dc(blo) around. (12 sts)
Round 13: [2dc in next st, 1dc] 6 times. (18 sts)

Legs:
Round 14: Miss 8 sts, insert hook into next st, yrh, draw yarn through both loops on hook, 8dc (makes first leg).
Round 15: 8dc.
Round 16: [Dc2tog, 1dc] twice, dc2tog. (6 sts)
Fasten off yarn, leaving a 10cm (4in) tail.
Rejoin yarn to second leg-hole. Dc one round, then rep Rounds 15 and 16.
Fasten off.

HAIR
Round 1: Using yarn A, 2ch, 6dc in 2nd ch from hook, ss in first dc to join, pm. (6 sts)
Round 2: 2dc in each st around. (12 sts)
Round 3: Ch3, 1htr in next st, 1tr in each of next 6 sts, 1htr (leave rem 4 sts unworked).
Fasten off, leaving a 7.5cm (3in) end and set aside.

CAP
Round 1: Using yarn E, 2ch, 6dc in first ch, ss in first dc to join, pm.
Round 2: 2dc in each st around. (12 sts)

Row 3: 3ch, 3tr in next st, ss in next st, leaving rem 9 sts unworked.
Fasten off.

FINISHING
To make the wired legs and arms follow the instructions on page 125, using yarns B and C to wrap arms, E for legs and A for feet.
Stitch hair and cap to top of head, using the yarn tails.

Braces:
Using yarn D, ss in any st at left-hand side front of Round 12, 12ch, take ch over shoulder, ss in any st on right-hand side of back. Fasten off yarn.
Rep on other side to make second brace.
To make lederhosen, embroider a chain stitch (see pages 122–123) from right brace to left in a straight line. Weave in ends.

Embroidery:
Embroider eyes, nose as for Gretel, use a brown or neutral thread to embroider the mouth.

Skill level: ★★★

Size

21.5cm (8½in) tall (including hat)

You will need

- DK (light worsted) yarn:
  50g (1¾oz) each of black (A) and
  purple (C)
  25g (⅞oz) of pale green (B)
  20g (¾oz) of deep pink (D)
  Small amounts of grey (E), orange
  and brown
  10g (⅜oz) of metallic black or silver
  (optional)
- 3mm (US D/3) crochet hook
- Removable stitch marker
- Toy filling
- Tapestry needle
- Medium gauge wire – one 35cm
  (13¾in) length; one 12.5cm (5in)
  length

Abbreviations

blo	back loop only
ch	chain
cont	continue
dc	double crochet
dc2tog	double crochet two sts together
flo	front loop only
htr	half treble
pm	place marker
rep	repeat
rem	remaining
ss	slip stitch
st(s)	stitch(es)
t-ch	turning chain
tr	treble
tr2tog	treble two sts together
tr5tog	treble five sts together

WICKED WITCH

Who is this lovely old lady, so friendly and welcoming to Hansel and Gretel?
It's a shame that they have always lived in the forest – if they were more streetwise,
they might see through her grin and notice the witch's hat and broomstick!

WITCH

Hat:

Worked in a spiral.

Using yarn A, 2ch, 6dc in 2nd ch from hook, ss in
first dc to join. (6 sts)

Rounds 1–5: Pm, dc around.

Round 6: [2dc in next st, 1dc] 3 times. (9 sts)

Rounds 7–10: Dc around.

Round 11: 2dc in first st, [2dc in next st, 1dc]
4 times. (14 sts)

Round 12: Dc around.

Brim:

Round 13: 2ch (counts as 1htr now and
throughout), 1htr in base of ch, 2htr in each st
around, ss in 2nd ch of t-ch to join. (28 sts)

Round 14: 1ch, dc around, ss in first dc to join.
(28 sts)

Fasten off yarn A, weave in ends.

Stuff hat with toy filling.

Face and hair:

Round 15: Join yarn B to blo of Round 12,
dc(blo) around. (14 sts)

Rounds 16–19: Dc around.

Round 20: 3ch, 5tr in next st (to make a nose),
13dc.

Round 21: Work 1 dc in the base of the 3ch and
1dc in the base of the 5tr from Round 20, dc
across. (14 sts)

Round 22: Rep Round 20 (for chin).

Round 23: Work 1 dc in the base of the 3ch and
1dc in the base of the 5tr from Round 22, dc
across. (14 sts)

Special abbreviation

Loop stitch – insert hook in next st,
wrap yarn twice (or more if longer
loops are preferred) around index finger
of hand controlling yarn. Holding loops
securely on finger, yrh, bring to front of
work and work 1dc in next st. Release
loop from finger. Rep for each loop st
worked.

Tips

Due to the weight of the witch and her spindly legs she will stand up more securely if supported by her broomstick.

For a simpler skirt, skip Round 31 and move straight to Round 32.

Round 24: [Dc2tog] 7 times. (7 sts)
Fasten off yarn B, leaving a 10cm (4in) tail.
Stuff face with toy filling.

Body:

Move st marker to centre back (opposite nose and chin).
Round 25: Join yarn C at st marker, dc around. (7 sts)
Round 26: 3ch (counts as 1tr now and throughout), 1tr in base of ch, 2tr in each st around. (14 sts)
Round 27: 1ch, 2dc into each st across. (28 sts)

Armhole set-up:

Round 28: 4dc, miss 5 sts, 9dc, miss 5 sts, 5dc (makes two armholes of 5 sts each and a central body of 18 sts).

Torso:

Rounds 29–30: Dc around centre 18 sts only.

Skirt:

Round 31 (stripe round): Attach yarn D at st marker, [2dc(flo) in next 2 sts, 2htr(flo) in next st, miss 1 st, 5tr(flo) in next st, miss 1 st, 2htr(flo) in next st, 2dc(flo) in next 2 sts] twice. (28 sts)
Fasten off yarn D and weave in ends.
Join metallic yarn to any st in Round 31, 1ch, dc around, ss to first dc to join. Fasten off. Weave in ends.
Round 32: Pick up yarn C at Round 30 (under stripe round). Dc(blo) around. (18 sts)
Round 33: 3ch [2tr in each of next 2 sts, 1tr] 5 times, 2 tr into each of next 2 sts. (30 sts)

Round 34: 3ch, tr across, ss in 3rd ch of t-ch to join.
Round 35 (stripe round): Join yarn D, leaving yarn C attached at back of work. With yarn D, dc(flo) around, ss in first dc to join. (30 sts)
Fasten off yarn D.
Round 36: With yarn C, dc(blo) around, ss in first dc to join. (30 sts)
Round 37: 3ch, 1tr in base of ch, [1tr, 2tr in next st, 2tr, 2tr in next st] 5 times, 1tr, 2tr in next st, 2tr, ss in 3rd ch of t-ch to join. (42 sts)
Rounds 38–39: Rep Rounds 35–36.

Scallop hem:

[1dc in first st, miss 1 st, 5tr in next st, miss 1 st, 2dc] 7 times.
Fasten off yarn C and weave in ends.
Join silver/metallic yarn to any st of scallop hem, 1ch, dc around, ss to first dc to join.
Fasten off and weave in ends.

Arms:

Rejoin yarn C to armpit join.
Round 1: 1ch, dc around. (5 sts)
Rounds 2–5: Dc around.
Fasten off yarn C.

SKIRT BASE

Round 1: Using yarn A, 6ch, ss in first ch to join, 3ch, 13tr into ring, ss in 3rd ch of t-ch to join. (14 sts)
Rounds 2–3: 3ch, 1tr in base of ch, 2tr in each st around, ss in 3rd ch of t-ch to join. (56 sts)
Fasten off yarn A, leaving a 30cm (12in) tail.

CLOAK

(Worked bottom up)
Row 1: Using yarn A, 27ch, 1tr in 4th st from hook and in each ch across. (24 sts)
Rows 2–9: 3ch, tr across. (24 sts)
Row 10: 2ch, 1tr in next st (counts as tr2tog), tr2tog 12 times. (12 sts)
Leave yarn A attached.

Ribbon:

Using orange yarn, 20ch, dc across 12 sts of Row 10, 20ch.
Fasten off orange yarn. Weave ends into chain.

Cloak edging:

Picking up yarn A, work edging down the longer edge of the cloak as follows:
5ch, 2dc around stem of tr; rep from * to corner, 3dc in corner, **5ch, miss 1dc, 2dc; rep from ** to next corner, 3dc, rep from * to *, 5ch, 2dc around 3 ch at end of row, repeat from * to * until you reach the last row.
Fasten off yarn A.

FINISHING

Fill body and skirt with toy stuffing.

Legs:

Using the longer piece of wire, make the legs as in step 4 on page 125. Place feet through centre of skirt base and push base up inside skirt. When you are happy with the position, stitch the base to the inside of the skirt. Using yarn A, stitch up through base and round wire inside several times to secure it, then wrap yarn A around each piece of wire down to foot covering all exposed wire. Stitch through each foot several times to keep in place.

Hands:

Join yarn B to any st at end of arm, 1ch, 5dc , *4ch, turn and dc in each ch, ss in next st, ch5, turn and dc in each ch, ss in next st; rep from * twice more, 4ch, dc in each ch.
Fasten off yarn. Weave in ends.
Rep for other arm.

Shoes:

Using yarn A, 2ch, 6dc in 2nd ch from hook to join. (6 sts)
Rounds 1–6: Dc around.
Round 7: 4dc, turn (leaving rem 2 sts unworked).
Row 8: Dc across.
Fasten off.

Rep for second shoe.
Place foot inside shoe and use tail to stitch to shoe to ankle.

Hair:

Row 1: Using yarn E, 11ch, miss first ch, 1dc in each ch across. (10 sts)
Row 2: 1ch, work 1 loop st in each st to end.
Row 3: 1ch, dc across. (10 sts)
Rep Rows 2–3 once more. Fasten off, leave a 10cm (4in) tail. Use tail to attach hair under hat.

Broomstick:

Using brown yarn, make a tassel by wrapping yarn around three fingers about 15 times, thread end of yarn into tapestry needle and stitch round and through top of loops. Slide the loops off your fingers. Make another stitch around and through centre of yarn approximately 1.5cm (⅝in) from the top. Tighten and wrap around several more times and cut through loops at bottom.

Push the 12.5cm (5in) piece of wire through centre of tassel at widest part. Bend over ends to make a hooked loop at each end. Fold bottom end over at right angles and check height against witch to make sure that it will create a tripod effect and enable the witch to stand up. Wrap brown yarn around the wire, covering it from top through tassel to base, positioning tassel to cover the foot at end of broom and stitching in place. Attach broomstick to one of the witch's hands and dress with a couple of stitches.

Embroidery:

See pages 122–123 for details of embroidery stitches. Using sparkly yarn, stitch five stars to back (RS) of cloak. Wrap cloak around witch's shoulders and tie in a cute bow under her chin. Using black thread make two eyes with French knots and in between the nose and the chin embroider a couple of stitches in red thread for a mouth.

Tip

The fingers will be quite twisty and floppy so stitch in position onto the dress on one side, then attach the other hand to the broomstick and attach both to the other side of dress. If you wish you can pin them out into a hand shape and spray with fabric stiffener to make them more rigid.

"Nibble, nibble like a mouse, Who is nibbling on my house?"

Skill level: ★ / ★★

Size

16.5 x 13 x 19cm (6½ x 5¼ x 7½in)

You will need

- DK (light worsted) yarn:
  50g (1¾oz) of light brown (A)
  30g (1oz) each of ginger or tan (B)
  and white (C)
  Small amounts of pastel, cream, pink,
  red, green and grey
- 3mm (US D/3) crochet hook
- Tapestry needle
- Embroidery thread or 2ply yarn in
  different colours
- Felt – 20cm (8in) squares of black or
  navy and pink
- Assortment of coloured felts, buttons,
  ribbons and braid
- Fusible interfacing (optional)
- Toy stuffing

Abbreviations

blo	back loop only
ch	chain
cont	continue
dc	double crochet
dc2tog	double crochet two sts together
dtr	double treble
flo	front loop only
htr	half treble
lp(s)	loop(s)
rep	repeat
ss	slip stitch
st(s)	stitch(es)
t-ch	turning chain
tr	treble

GINGERBREAD COTTAGE

This charming scene setter or decoration is made in separate pieces and assembled together at the end. You can really let loose for the decoration on the façade of the house, with cute, colourful buttons, beads and scraps of felt and trimmings to emulate a candy-covered cottage… But creep around the back and you will see that all is not as it seems; push past the cobwebs, mind that enormous spider – and who on earth could have left their broomstick lying around like that!

FRONT AND BACK

Row 1: Using yarn A, 26ch, 1dc in 2nd ch from hook, dc in each ch across, turn. (25 sts)
Rows 2–10: 1ch, dc across, turn.
Row 11: 1ch, miss 1 dc, 21dc, dc2tog, turn. (23 sts)
Row 12: 1ch, miss 1 dc, 19dc, dc2tog, turn. (21 sts)
Row 13: 1ch, miss 1 dc, 17dc, dc2tog, turn. (19 sts)
Row 14: 1ch, miss 1 dc, 15dc, dc2tog, turn. (17 sts)
Row 15: 1ch, miss 1 dc, 13dc, dc2tog, turn. (15 sts)
Row 16: 1ch, miss 1 dc, 11dc, dc2tog, turn. (13 sts)
Row 17: 1ch, miss 1 dc, 9dc, dc2tog, turn. (11 sts)
Row 18: 1ch, miss 1 dc, 7dc, dc2tog, turn. (9 sts)
Row 19: 1ch, miss 1 dc, 5dc, dc2tog, turn. (7 sts)
Row 20: 1ch, miss 1 dc, 3dc, dc2tog, turn. (5 sts)
Row 21: 1ch, miss 1 dc, 1dc, dc2tog, turn. (3 sts)
Work 3dc in 2nd st from hook, rotate work slightly and edge the fabric by working 1dc in each st on all sides, working 3dc in the corner stitches, ss in first dc of initial 3dc corner to join. This edging makes the finishing and seaming easier.

SIDES AND BASE

(make 3)
Follow pattern for Front and Back to Row 10.
Fasten off and weave in ends.

Row 1: Using yarn A, 26ch, 1dc in 2nd ch from hook, dc across, turn. (25 sts)
Rows 2–9: 1ch, dc across, turn. (25 sts)
Row 10: 1ch, dc across to last st, 3dc in last st, rotate work edge as for the Front and Back sections, finishing by working a ss in the first dc of 3dc corner.
Fasten off.

ROOF

Using yarn B, ch27. Starting at the ridge in centre of roof, the first side is worked from ridge to last row of scallops, you will then fasten off yarn and re-attach yarn to Row 2 to work on other side of roof.
Row 1: With yarn B, 27ch, 1htr in 3rd ch from hook, htr in each ch across. (25 sts)
Row 2: 2ch (counts as 1htr now and throughout), htr across, turn. (25 sts)

Scallop pattern:
*Row 3: 3ch, [miss 1 st, 5tr in next st, miss 1 st, ss in next 2 sts] 5 times along row, turn. (5 scallops)
Row 4: 3ch, 1tr(flo) in each st of Row 2.
Row 5: 3ch, 2tr in base of ch, miss 1 st, ss in next 2 sts, [miss 1 st, 5tr in next st, miss 1 st, ss in next 2 sts] 3 times, miss 1 st, 3tr in last st, turn.
Rep Rows 3–5 twice more.
Fasten off. Weave in ends. *
Rep for other side of roof as follows:
With yarn B, ss in back loop of first st in Row 2, 3ch, htr(blo) across, turn.
Rep from * to *.

Iced edging:

You will work around edge of both roof sections first and then work along each edge of each scallop row separately.

Using yarn C, ss in first ch of base chain (ridge of roof), 1ch, 24dc, 3dc in last st, dc in each side loop of rows in first roof section, 3dc in last side loop. Continue to work 1dc in side loops of rows on other side of roof section until you have worked back up to the base chain ridge, rep around other side of other roof section.

Fasten off yarn C.

Rejoin yarn C to first st of scallop row and the work scallop edge as follows:

[2dc, 3dc in centre st of each scallop, 2dc] around each scallop to end of row. Rep for each scallop row.

Fasten off, leaving a 7.5cm (3in) tail.

FINISHING

Block out wall and base pieces gently, making sure pieces have a neat squared edge.

When the pieces are dry, take a contrasting colour DK and seam outside edges together by working dc through side loops of rows on each piece, creating a neat raised edge. You could work a line of chain st if preferred.

Fasten off and weave in ends.

Fill the house with toy stuffing. This can make the house look rounded so it can be useful to pinch the wall sides together and stitch them in place to make the edges more pronounced. Using yarn A, attach roof piece to walls by carefully stitching walls to underside of roof.

Windows:

Cut seven 3 x 4cm (1¼ x 1½in) rectangles from black or navy felt. At top corners of each rectangle cut off a 1cm (⅜in) triangle to make a centre point. Cut seven 5 x 6cm (2 x 2¼in) rectangles from pink felt and shape the top as before. Place each dark window on a pink window and either sew in place with black cotton or stick with glue.

With a cream or white embroidery thread (or 2ply yarn) carefully stitch across the black felt in a diagonal grid, leaving about 1cm (⅜in) between lines. When working stitches in other direction, weave the needle over and under the previous

Tips

You can really go mad with decorating the front of the house with cute buttons or beads – you may find some that look exactly like sweets and candy.

On the back of the cottage it becomes obvious that not all is as it seems – stitch brown and beige small random shapes to the surface.

When blocking you can use spray starch or a fabric stiffening spray to make the shape more rigid when constructed.

stitches to create a diamond window pane effect. For the decorative window box, cut five 1.5 × 5cm (⅝ × 2in) pink felt strips and three 0.5 × 5cm (¼ × 2in) green felt strips. I have used pinking shears to make a zigzag top on the green strip. Cut two 0.5 × 5cm (¼ × 2in) strips from grey or brown felt with a zigzag top edge.

Stitch or stick the green strips to one side of a pink strip to look like plants growing in the window box, then stitch or stick to the bottom of three windows. Repeat with grey and pink strips for two windows and just pink strips for the last two.

On the front, attach the three windows with greenery in window boxes, two about 6 rows up from the bottom of the house and about 3 sts in from each side, and a third window about 2 rows down from the centre point. Attach a window with a plain window box on either side of house. On the back, add the two windows with grey strips leaving space for a door between.

Front door:

Row 1: Using yarn in the colour of your choice, 8ch, dc in 2nd ch from hook, 1dc in each ch to end, turn. (7 sts)

Rows 2–12: 1ch, dc across, turn.

Row 13: 3ch, miss 2 sts, [1tr, 3ch] twice in next st, ss in last st.

Fasten off and weave in the ends.

Cut a 3cm (1¼in) diameter semi-circle of black felt, place behind last row and st in place with black thread, or glue if preferred. This forms the decorative window arch.

Attach door to front of house between two lower windows.

Love hearts:

(make two or more)

Round 1: Using red yarn, 2ch, 8dc in 2nd ch from hook, ss in first dc to make a ring. (8 sts)

Round 2: Ss in next st, 2htr in each of next 3 sts, 2tr in each of next 3 sts, 1tr into next st, 1dtr in next st, 3ch, 2tr in each of next 3 sts, 2htr in each of next 3 sts, ss to join round.

Fasten off.

Attach two hearts above windows on front of house using tails.

Back of house:

Stitch on a piece of brown felt with ragged edges to make a ramshackle door and add a French knot (see pages 122–123 for embroidery stitches) in black yarn for a door knob.

Cobweb and spider:

Round 1: Using grey (a finer weight yarn with the same hook is fine), 5ch, ss into first ch to join.

Round 2: 3ch, 6tr in ring, ss in 3rd ch of t-ch to join.

Fasten off.

For the spider, make two French knots in black next to each other, then embroider 8 backstitches out from the knots as legs. It looks more spidery if worked at the edge of the web.

Cobweb strands:

Join yarn with a ss into any st under corner of roof, 1dc in each st along join of house front and roof (along edge of roof and up into the pointed gable and down the other edge). The exact number of sts is not important, but should not pucker the fabric. Ss in other roof corner, turn, [3ch, miss 2 or 3 sts, 1tr in next st] to the end of roof on the other side, ss into any st in corner of roof. This can be as freeform as you like.

Fasten off. Weave in ends.

Skill level: ★★

Size
Square: 16 x 16cm (6¼ x 6¼in)
Lollipop Trees (in pots): 10cm (4in) tall
Candy Canes (in pots): 13cm (5in) tall

You will need
- DK (light worsted) yarn:
  25g (¾oz) of greens (A)
  Oddments of pink (B), white (C), light
  brown (D) and red (E)
- 3mm (US D/3) crochet hook
- 2 removable stitch markers
- 2cm (¾in) diameter circles of felt –
  three cream, two pale pink
- Tapestry needle
- Embroidery thread or 2ply yarn in
  brown and white/cream
- Sewing needle
- Medium gauge wire – three 10cm
  (4in) lengths
- Toy stuffing
- Assortment of felts, beads and buttons

Abbreviations

beg	beginning
blo	back loop only
ch	chain
ch sp	chain space
cont	continue
dc	double crochet
htr	half treble
rep	repeat
rem	remaining
RH	right hand
ss	slip stitch
st(s)	stitch(es)
t-ch	turning chain
tr	treble
WS	wrong side

WITCH'S GARDEN

The witch's garden pieces are all made separately so that you can move them around and place them where you like. The crochet is simple – the pieces are mostly in double crochet. The teeny tiny bunting looks good arranged along the trees to mark a boundary to the garden area.

FRONT GARDEN
Using any shade of A, make 5ch, join to first ch with a ss to make a ring.
Round 1: 3ch (counts as first tr now and throughout), 2tr into ring *2ch, 3tr in ring rep from * 2 more times, 1htr into 3rd ch of t-ch to join.
Round 2: 3ch, 2tr into same ch sp, 1ch, *3tr, 2ch, 3tr in next ch sp, 1ch (working a corner); rep from * 2 more times, 3tr in ch sp, 1htr into 3rd ch of t-ch to join.
Round 3: 3ch, 2tr into same ch sp, 1ch, *3tr in next ch sp, 1ch, [3tr, 2ch, 3tr] in next corner ch sp, 1ch; rep from * 2 more times, 3tr in next ch sp, 1ch, 3tr in next corner ch sp, 1htr into 3rd ch of t-ch to join.
Round 4: 3ch, 2tr into same ch sp, 1ch, [3tr, 1ch] in each ch sp to corner ch sp, *[3tr, 2ch, 3tr in corner ch sp], 1ch, [3tr, 1ch] in each ch sp to corner ch sp; rep from * 2 more times, 3tr in last corner ch sp, 1htr into 3rd ch of t-ch to join.
Rep Round 4 five more times (for a total of nine rounds).

Change colour at each round or work all in one colour as desired.
Fasten off yarn.
Weave in ends neatly.
Block if desired.
Stitch the cream and pink circles of felt across centre of square in contrasting thread as a stepping stone path to the front door.

LOLLIPOP TREES
Using yarn C, make a magic ring, 3ch (counts as 1dc now and throughout), 7dc in ring, join with ss, place st marker in first st. (8 sts)
Change to B, 1ch, 1dc in back loop only of first st, *1dc(blo) in next st, 2dc(blo) in next st; rep from * to end, join to first st with ss. Move st marker. (12 sts)
Change to C, 1ch, *1dc(blo) in next 2 sts, *2dc(blo) in next st, 1dc in each of next 2 sts; rep from * to st marker; join to first st with ss. Move st marker.
Rep last round three more times, alternating between yarns B and C as set and increasing number of dcs worked between 2-dc increases by 1 each round, as set.
Fasten off yarn, leaving a long thread, cut and weave in other ends.
Make two spirals for each tree.

Tip

To keep your trees from tumbling over, you could place a weight inside the pot; a pebble, small coin or a curtain weight is ideal.

Make as many of the Lollipop Trees and Candy Canes as you want to place around the Witch's Garden.

CANDY CANE

Using yarn C, make 41ch.

Row 1: Miss first ch, *1dc into rem ch across, turn. (40 sts)

Row 2: 1ch (does not count as a dc now and throughout), rep Row 1 from * across. (40 sts)

Row 3: Change to B, 1ch, 1dc into each st to end, turn. (40 sts)

Rep Row 3 once more.

Fasten off yarn leaving a long tail.

BASE

Pot:

(make 2 in yarn D, 1 in yarn E)

Round 1: *Using required colour, 5ch, ss to first ch to join into a ring, 3ch, 11tr in ring, ss to join.** Place marker.

Round 2: 1ch, 1dc(blo) in each st around to marker. Do not ss to join, but instead move marker to last st worked to indicate the end of the round.

Rep Round 2 twice more.

Fasten off, leaving a long tail. Pull tail from start of work into the pot – no need to weave in the end.

Grass circle:

(make 3)

Using A, rep from * to ** of Round 1 of Pot pattern.

Round 2: 3ch, 1tr in base of ch, 2tr in each st, ss in top of 3rd ch to join round.

Fasten off, and weave in ends.

BUNTING

(make 10 in assorted colours)

Flowers: Using required colour, 2ch, *[3ch, 1dc] into first ch; rep from * 4 more times, 3ch, ss to second ch of ch2 to join.

Fasten off and weave in ends.

Cord:

Using yarn A, 6ch, ss into 3rd ch from hook to make a loop, 3ch, *insert hook through ch sp (petal) in flower, ss to join, 3ch; rep from * to attach each flower. When all flowers are attached, 3ch, ss to 3rd ch from hook to make another loop.

Fasten off and weave in ends.

FINISHING

Lollipop trees:

Wrap two lengths of wire in yarn C (see page 126).

Stitch trunk to WS of one Lollipop.

Add second Lollipop to sandwich wire and stitch together using yarn B.

Place a little toy stuffing into each Pot.

Insert wrapped wire stem into centre of one Grass circle. On WS, bend end of wire over and stitch in place using the tail (you may need to go over the stitching a few times to get tree to stay upright).

Place a Lollipop tree and Grass circle in each yarn D Pot and stitch in place using the long tail. Fasten off. Thread tail through pot, hiding the ends.

Candy cane:

Wrap the candy cane strip around the third length of wire, stitching into place. Stitch ends securely to cover wire.

Bend over like a hook at one end.

Push straight end of covered Candy Cane through the centre of a Grass circle, stitching through to hold in place using the long tail. Stitch Candy Cane and Grass circle inside yarn E Pot, using the long tail. Fasten off. Thread the tail through the pot, hiding the ends.

Skill level: ★

Size

Approx 26cm (10¼in) from base to top

You will need

- DK (light worsted) yarn:
  Small amounts of dark brown, beige
  and green
- 3mm (US D/3) crochet hook
- Medium gauge wire – approx 60cm
  (23½in) length
- Pliers
- Wire cutters
- Tapestry needle
- Air-drying clay
- Felt circle, approx 6.5cm (2½in)
  diameter in brown or green
- PVA glue

Abbreviations

ch	chain
dc	double crochet
ss	slip stitch
st(s)	stitch(es)
tr	treble
t-ch	turning chain

Tip

These look really effective in groups of
different heights and widths, positioned
around the Gingerbread Cottage to
make a creepy clearing!

SILVER BIRCH TREES

These simple-to-make scene setters are created using
lengths of wire and scraps of brown and beige yarn, with just a
sturdy pair of pliers, wire and yarn. The crochet grassy base adds
the finishing touch.

GRASS

Base ring: Using green yarn, 6ch, ss in first ch to
make a ring. Ch1, 12dc in ring, ss in first dc to
join. (12 sts)
Round 1: 3ch (counts as 1tr now and
throughout), 1tr in same st, 2tr in each st to end,
ss in 3rd ch of t-ch to join. (24 sts)
Round 2: Rep Round 1. (48 sts)
Round 3: 3ch, 1tr in each st to end, ss in 3rd ch
of t-ch to join.
Fasten off, leaving a 30cm (12in) tail.

TREE

Cut a 44cm (17¼in) length of wire and bend the
last 17cm (6¾in) to meet the larger section. Twist,
starting at the bent end, for approximately 8cm
(3¼in) to form the trunk, then pull the ends
apart at the top to start forming a couple of
branches. Twist smaller lengths of wire onto the
main wires to emulate tree branches.
Thread a tapestry needle with brown yarn and
stitch through the loop at the bottom of the
trunk to attach. Draw the yarn through and stitch
round the end of the looped wire several times.
Wrap the yarn around the trunk and branches
until there are no gaps of wire left visible.
Stitch through at the end and fasten off.
Change to beige yarn and, with the tapestry
needle, make a few stitches into the brown yarn
to attach. Wind the beige yarn round the tree
neatly, leaving a few gaps at intervals to expose
the brown yarn bark below. Once you are happy
with the coverage, stitch through to secure and
fasten off.

BASE

Roll a 10cm (4in) ball of air-
drying clay in the palm of
your hand.
Place on a ceramic or plastic
plate or tray and press down
to make a dome with a flat
base.
Stick the yarn wrapped
trunk down into the clay for
about 2cm (1in) then
remove and leave the clay to
dry for 24 hours.
Cover the clay base with the
crochet grass, ensuring the
central hole lines up
with the
hole for the
trunk. Place the
felt circle under
the base and attach
to the grass using the long tail. Fasten off.

FINISHING

Carefully put a drop of glue into the hole made by
the wire, insert the tree trunk into the centre of
the Grass. Push down securely and leave to dry.

Skill level: ★

Size

16.5cm (6½in) tall (excluding hood)

You will need

- DK (light worsted) yarn:
  10g (⅜oz) of ginger or orange (A)
  20g (¾oz) each of flesh tone (B) and
  medium blue (C)
  Small amount of white (D)
  30g (1oz) of red (E)
  Small amount of black (F)
  10g (⅜oz) of golden yellow
  Small amount of brown and white
- 3mm (US D/3) crochet hook
- Removable stitch marker
- Toy stuffing
- Tapestry needle
- Small amount of black and red
  embroidery thread or 2ply yarn
- Medium gauge wire – one 15cm (6in)
  length; two 7.5cm (3in) lengths
- 3 small red beads (optional)

Abbreviations

blo	back loop only
ch	chain
ch sp	chain space
cont	continue
dc	double crochet
dc2tog	double crochet two sts together
htr	half treble crochet
rem	remaining
ss	slip stitch
st(s)	stitch(es)
t-ch	turning chain
tr	treble

RED RIDING HOOD

This cute figure of Red Riding Hood is worked mostly in a spiral in double crochet, using stitch markers. She has little black boots and a removable bright red hood and cape. Over one arm, she has a basket of cherry cakes to take to Granny's house, which is a cute little make too! Due to the wire arms and legs she is not suitable for small children.

HEAD AND BODY

Base ring: Using yarn B, 2ch, 9dc in 2nd ch, ss in first dc to join. (9 sts)
Round 1: Place st marker. 2dc in each st around. (18 sts)
Rounds 2–8: Dc around.
Fill head with toy stuffing.
Round 9: [Dc2tog] 9 times. (9 sts)
Fasten off yarn B, leaving a 7.5cm (3in) tail.
Fill rest of head with toy stuffing.

Body:

Round 10: Using yarn C, 1dc(blo) into each back loop to end of round. (9 sts)
Round 11: 2dc in each st around. (18 sts)
Round 12: 3dc, [2dc in next st, 2dc] 4 times, 3dc. (22 sts)

Armholes and waist:

Round 13: 4dc, miss 4 sts, 6dc, miss 4 sts, 4dc (makes two armholes of 4 sts each and a body of 14 sts). Cont to work into 14 sts in centre only as follows:
Rounds 14–15: Dc around. (14 sts)
Fill body to waist with stuffing.

Skirt:

Round 16: 2dc in first st, 12dc, 2dc in last st. (16 sts)
Round 17: [3dc, 2dc in next st] 4 times. (20 sts)
Rounds 18–22: Dc around. (20 sts)
Round 23: [2dc in next st, 9dc] twice. (22 sts)
Rounds 14–28: Dc around.
Ss in first dc to join. (22 sts)
Fasten off yarn C, leaving a 7.5cm (3in) tail.
Fill skirt with toy stuffing.

Frilled hem:

Using yarn D, ss in any st of Round 28 to join, [3ch, ss in next st] around. (11 chain loops around hem of skirt)
Fasten off yarn D, leaving a 7.5cm (3in) tail.

Arms:

Round 1: Using yarn C, place st marker at join of armpit, 2dc into join of armpit and body (no stitch present), then work 1dc in each of next 4 free sts. (6 sts)
Rounds 2–5: Dc around. (6 sts)
Fill arms with little bits of toy stuffing as you work.
Round 6: [2dc in next st, 2dc] twice. (8 sts)
Round 7: Dc around, ss in first dc to join.
Fasten off yarn C, leaving a 7.5cm (3in) tail.

Hands:
Round 8: With yarn B, dc(blo) around. (6 sts)
Round 9: Dc around, ss in first dc to join. (6 sts)
Fasten off yarn B. Use tail and tapestry needle to stitch through all 6 sts to tighten into a hand shape. Weave in all ends.
Repeat for other arm.

SKIRT BASE
Base ring: Using yarn C, 5ch, ss in first ch to join. (5 sts)
Round 1: 3ch (counts as a t-ch now and throughout), 9tr in ring, ss in 3rd ch of t-ch to join. (10 sts)
Round 2: 3ch, 1tr in base of ch, 2tr in each st around, ss in 3rd ch of t-ch to join. (20 sts)
Fasten off, leaving a 15cm (6in) tail.

APRON
Base chain: Using yarn D, 22ch, place st marker, 27ch.
Fasten off yarn D, leaving a 7.5cm (3in) tail.
Row 1: Re-attach yarn D at st marker (22nd ch). Working into the longer (27 ch) section, 5dc, turn. (5 sts)
Rows 2–5: 1ch, 5dc. (5 sts)
Row 6: 1ch, miss next st, 5tr in next st, miss next st, 1dc.
Fasten off yarn D.
Weave in all ends.
Tie apron around waist of figure.

HAIR
Base ring: Using yarn A, 2ch, 6dc in 2nd ch, ss in first dc to join. (6 sts)
Round 1: 1ch, 2dc in each st around, ss in first dc to join. (12 sts)
Round 2: 1ch, (1dc, 2dc in next st) 6 times, ss in first dc to join. (18 sts)
Round 3: 3ch, 11tr, turn (leaving rem 6 sts unworked). (12 sts)

Bunches:
Worked in rows as follows:
Row 4: 3ch, 11tr, *[5ch, ss in base of ch] 3 times* in base of last tr.
Fasten off yarn A, leaving 7.5cm (3in) tail.
Re-attach yarn at other end of Row 4 (at the base of the first tr) and rep from * to * making the other bunch.
Fasten off yarn A, weave in ends.

HOODED CAPE
Hood:
Worked from point of hood down, in a spiral until instructed to work in rounds.
Base ring: Using yarn E, 2ch, 6dc in second ch, ss in first dc to join.
Rounds 1–3: Place st marker, dc around. (6 sts)
Round 4: [2dc in next st, 1dc] 3 times. (9 sts)
Round 5: Dc around.
Round 6: [2dc in next st, 2dc] 3 times. (12 sts)
Round 7: Dc around.
Round 8: [2dc in next st, 1dc] 6 times. (18 sts)
Round 9: 2dc, [2dc in next st, 1dc] 8 times, ss in first dc to join. (26 sts)
Work in rounds as follows:
Round 10: 3ch, [2tr, 2tr in next st] 8 times, 1tr, ss in 3rd ch of t-ch to join. (34 sts)
Round 11: 3ch, 1tr in base of ch, [3tr, 2tr in next st] 8 times, 2tr in last st, ss in 3rd ch of t-ch to join. (44 sts)
Round 12: 3ch, tr around, ss in 3rd ch of t-ch to join. (44 sts)

Cape:
Round 13: 3ch, 11tr into each of next 11 sts, turn (leaving rem 32 sts unworked). (12 sts)
Round 14: 3ch, 2tr in each st across, turn. (23 sts)
Round 15: [3ch, miss next st, 1dc in next st] 11 times, turn. (11 3-ch loops)
Round 16: 6ch, (counts as first tr and 3ch,) 1dc in next ch sp, [3ch, miss next st, 1dc in next ch sp] 10 times, 3ch, 1tr in last st. (12 ch loops.)
Fasten off yarn E. Weave in ends.

Ties:

Using yarn E, leaving a 7.5cm (3in) tail at beg, make 2 chains of 30, fasten off each chain, leaving a 7.5cm (3in) tail.

Using ends and tapestry needle, stitch one chain to each end of Round 1 and weave in ends neatly. Put cape onto Red Riding Hood with the hood at the back and tie chains in a bow under chin at front.

LEGS

Take the 15cm (6in) length of wire and bend into legs as in step 4 on page 125.

Place loop inside skirt and put toy stuffing around wire legs. With a length of yarn F and tapestry needle, stitch wire to toy stuffing to hold in place. Insert wire legs through base and (using tail of yarn C), stitch base to inside skirt covering the stuffing.

Bend each wire end over to make a foot loop.

Using yarn F, wrap yarn around each wire leg as described on page 125.

Bend foot loops up at right angles to stand the figure up.

BASKET

Base ring: Using yellow yarn, 4ch, ss in first ch to join.

Round 1: 1ch, 10dc in ring, ss in first dc to join. (10 sts)

Round 2: 2ch (counts as 1htr), 1htr in base of ch, 2htr in each st around, ss in 2nd ch of t-ch to join. (20 sts)

Round 3: 2ch, 1htr(blo) around, ss in 2nd ch of t-ch to join. (20 sts)

Round 4: 2ch, htr around, ss in 2nd ch of t-ch to join. (20 sts)

Fasten off yarn, leaving a 7.5cm (3in) tail.

Handle:

Using the 7.5cm (3in) length of wire, bend two small loops at each end.

Using the yellow yarn and tapestry needle, wrap yarn around wire until fully covered, stitching through loops at each end several times to secure.

Fasten off yarn, leaving a 15cm (6in) tail.

Bend wire into a semi-circle shape.

Using the end and tapestry needle, stitch the handle to each side of the basket and weave in all ends.

Cherry cakes:

(make three)

Base ring: With yarn D, 2ch, 5dc in second ch, ss in first dc to join.

Fasten off yarn D, leaving a 7.5cm (3in) tail.

Rounds 1–3: Using brown yarn, and working in a spiral (with st marker if needed) dc in each st. Fasten off brown yarn and with tapestry needle and tail, stitch through all 6 sts and tighten into a rounder shape. Stitch through back of cake and trim ends.

FINISHING

Using tail of yarn A and a tapestry needle, stitch hair to top of head with a bunch at each side.

Embroidery:

Follow the instructions for embroidering a face on page 124. Use black embroidery thread for eyes, and make a couple of small stitches for a nose. I have chosen not to give her a mouth but you can embroider a mouth in red if you wish. To make the cherries, stitch a French knot (see page 122) in the centre of the white ring with a little red yarn or embroidery thread, or stitch a red bead in the same place if you prefer. Place finished cakes in basket.

Place basket over Red's arm and bend her arm upwards, stitch hand to dress to hold the basket in position.

Skill level: ★★ / ★★★

Size

20cm (8in) tall, ear to tail

You will need

- DK (light worsted) yarn:
  40g (1½oz) of pale grey (A)
  20g (¾oz) of deep red or
  burgundy (B)
  20g (¾oz) of charcoal or dark
  grey (C)
  10g (⅜oz) of black (D)
  Small amount of beige or light
  brown (E)
- Toy stuffing
- Medium gauge wire – one 30cm
  (12in) length; one 14cm (5½in) length
- 6 small metal or wooden beads
- Felt – two 1cm (⅜in) black or navy
  equilateral triangles; 1.5 × 1cm
  (⅝ × ⅜in) rectangle of orange
- 3mm (US D/3) crochet hook
- Removable stitch marker
- Tapestry needle
- Black embroidery thread or 2ply yarn
- Deep red or burgundy sewing thread
- Sewing needle

Abbreviations

blo	back loop only
ch	chain
ch sp	chain space
cont	continue
dc	double crochet
dc2tog	double crochet two sts together
htr	half treble
pm	place marker
rem	remaining
rep	repeat
ss	slip stitch
st(s)	stitch(es)
tr	treble
tr2tog	treble two sts together
yrh	yarn round hook

WICKED WOLF

My wolf is a bit of a rakish gentleman, some might say caddish! He is mostly made in spirals in double and treble crochet, using stitch markers. He stands up independently due to his wired legs and tail. This wily fellow thinks that he can charm Red Riding Hood into giving him the basket of cherry cakes that she has baked for her sick Granny and he is looking forward to a good meal (when he snaps Red up too!). I am not so sure because Red is quite a savvy girl – I think she can handle Mr Wolf.

HEAD AND BODY

Starting with the nose, work in a spiral using st marker to indicate beginning of rounds. Move the st marker as you work.

Base ring: Using yarn A, 2ch, 6dc in 2nd ch, ss in first dc to join. (6 sts)

Rounds 1–2: Pm, dc around.

Round 3: 2dc in each st around. (12 sts)

Round 4: [2dc in next st, 1dc] 6 times. (18 sts)

Round 5: Dc around.

Round 6: [2dc in next st, 1dc] 9 times. (27 sts)

Rounds 7–9: Dc around. (27 sts)

Ears:

Round 10: Pm, *[6ch, miss next st],* (first ear) ss in next 4 sts; rep from * to * once, (second ear), 1dc into each of rem 20 sts to end of round.

Round 11: *[3dc in next ear ch sp, ch3, 3dc in same ch sp]*, ss in next 4 sts; rep from * to * once more, 2dc, pm, turn, and cont in rows (leaving rem 20 sts unworked).

Shape back of head:

Row 1: 1ch, 10dc(blo), turn. (10 sts)

Row 2: 3ch (counts as 1 tr now and throughout), 9tr, turn. (10 sts)

Row 3: 3ch, miss next st, 6tr, tr2tog, turn. (8 sts)

Row 4: 3ch, miss next st, 4tr, tr2tog. (6 sts)

Rejoin back of head section to the rem sts in Round 10 as follows:

Round 12: Pm, miss next 5 free sts of Round 10, 10dc, miss next 5 sts, insert hook into 3rd ch at beg of Row 4, yrh and draw yarn through st, leaving 1 loop on hook.

You have now joined the back of the head to the rest of the head. (16 sts)

Resume working in a spiral as follows:

Neck:

Rounds 13–14: Dc around. (16 sts)

Fasten off yarn A, leaving a long tail to darn in sides of head shaping to close any gaps. Weave ends in.

Fill head with toy stuffing.

Shoulders:

Pm at centre back of neck, start rounds here.

Round 15: Using yarn B, dc around. (16 sts)

Round 16: 2dc in each of first 3 sts, [1dc, 2dc in each of next 2 sts] 4 times, 2dc in last st. (28 sts)

Armholes:

Round 17: 4dc, leave next 6 sts unworked, 8dc, leave next 6 sts unworked, 4dc (makes two armholes of 6 sts and a body of 16 sts). Cont to work into central 16 sts only.

Waistcoat:

Rounds 18–19: Dc around. (16 sts)

Round 20: [2dc in next st, 1dc] twice, [2dc, 3htr in next st] twice, 2dc, [2dc in next st, 1dc] twice. (24 sts)

Fasten off yarn B. Weave in ends. Fill body with toy stuffing.

Hips and legs:

Round 21: Attach yarn A to centre back st of Round 19 (under shaped hem of waistcoat). Dc around. (16 sts)

Round 22: 2ch (counts as 1htr now and throughout), 1htr in base of ch, 2htr in each st around, ss in 2nd ch of t-ch to join. (32 sts)

Rounds 23–24: 2ch, htr around, ss in 2nd ch of t-ch to join.

Round 25: [Dc2tog] twice, [2dc, dc2tog] 6 times, [dc2tog] twice. (22 sts)

Fill body with toy stuffing.

Legs:

Round 26: Insert hook into next st, miss next 10 sts, insert hook into next st, yrh, draw yarn through both sts leaving one loop on hook. This creates 2 leg-holes of 10 sts each. Cont to work 1dc into next free st of first leg-hole, pm, 9dc, work 2dc into join of leg. (12 sts)

Work leg as follows, filling with stuffing as you work every couple of rounds:

Leg rounds 1–4: Pm, dc around. (12 sts)

Leg round 5: [1dc, dc2tog] 4 times. (8 sts)

Leg round 6: [Dc2tog, 2dc] twice. (6 sts)

Leg round 7: [1dc, dc2tog] twice. (4 sts)

Leg rounds 8–17: Dc around.

Fasten off yarn A, leaving a 20cm (8in) tail. Re-attach yarn A to other leg-hole and rep for second leg.

"Why grandma, what big teeth you have got"

Arms:

Round 1: Attach yarn A at armpit join. 1dc, pm, dc around. (7 sts)

Rounds 2–3: Dc around. (7 sts)

Round 4: Dc2tog, 5dc. (6 sts)

Put a little toy stuffing into top of arm.

Round 5: Dc around. (6 sts)

Round 6: Dc2tog, 4dc. (5 sts)

Rounds 7–10: Dc around.

Fasten off yarn A, leaving a 7.5cm (3in) tail. Use tapestry needle and tail to stitch through last 5 sts drawing them into a tight circle. Weave in ends. Re-attach yarn at other armhole and rep for second arm.

TAIL

Base ring: Using yarn A, 2ch, 6dc in 2nd ch, ss in first dc to join. (6 sts)

Rounds 1–5: Pm, dc around. (6 sts)

Rounds 6: [1dc, 2dc in next st] 3 times. (9 sts)

Rounds 7–12: Dc around.

Round 13: [1dc, 2dc in next st] 4 times, 1dc. (13 sts)

Fill tail with stuffing as you work every couple of rounds.

Rounds 14–20: Dc around. (13 sts)

Round 21: 1dc, [dc2tog] 6 times. (7 sts)

Round 22: 1dc, [dc2tog] 3 times. (4 sts)

Fasten off yarn A, leaving a 20cm (8in) tail. Use tail to stitch through sts of Round 22. Weave in ends.

WIRING LEGS

Carefully insert 30cm (12in) piece of wire into end of leg at Round 17, ease wire up leg towards body and push through the other leg-hole so that each leg has wire protruding from the end. Check each end of wire against the length of the leg that you have made, trim ends to match length if necessary. Bend each wire end into a foot loop with pliers, then with tapestry needle and tails of yarn A, stitch the leg ends around the wire, wrapping yarn ends around foot and stitching through loop several times to secure the foot.

Bend foot upwards at a right angle to enable the wolf to stand up.

WIRING TAIL

With the 14cm (5½in) length of wire, insert wire through base of tail at last round and push up and out of the other end, make a small loop at both ends of wire end and using yarn A and tapestry needle, stitch ends tightly around wire to ensure that the wire stays inside tail.

Stitch top of tail to middle of wolf's bottom above join of legs and stitch through body and tail several times until the tail feels secure, weave in ends.

You can now move the tail into position, allowing the wolf to stand up unaided.

TOP HAT AND SCARF

Hat:

Base ring: Using yarn D, 2ch, 10dc in 2nd ch, ss in first dc to join. (10 sts)

Round 1: 2ch, 1htr in base of ch, 2htr in each st to end of round, ss in 2nd ch of t-ch to join. (20 sts)

Round 2: 2ch, 1htr (blo) around, ss in 2nd ch of t-ch to join.

Rounds 3–5: 2ch, htr around.

Brim:

Round 6: 3ch, 1tr in base of ch 2tr in each st around, ss in 3rd ch of t-ch to join. (40 sts)

Fasten off yarn D, leaving a 7.5cm (3in) tail.

Scarf:

Using yarn E, 59ch, 1tr in 4th ch from hook, 1tr in each ch to end. (46 sts)

Fasten off yarn E. Weave in ends.

Tie around wolf's neck.

FINISHING

Embroidery:

See pages 122–123 for details of embroidery stitches, and page 124 for instructions on stitching a face.

Using black yarn, make a large French knot at the end of the nose, or stitch on a black shiny button or bead.

With black embroidery thread or 2ply yarn, make 3 backstitches in a slight curve as a mouth and make 1 vertical straight stitch from mouth to nose.

Ears:

Using black thread stitch the triangles of black or navy felt to each of the wolf's ears. You can stick them on with glue if you prefer.

Eyes:

Cut the orange felt rectangle in half diagonally to make two long triangles and stitch or stick these onto the face on either side of nose, directly below each ear with the wider end in the centre. With a little black DK yarn and a tapestry needle, make a single black vertical stitch through centre of each triangle, stitch straight diagonal lines above each eye to make eyebrows, (pointing down in the centre).

Waistcoat:

Using sewing thread and a sewing needle, stitch 4 gold beads down the centre front.

Fur:

Using a length of yarn C and tapestry needle, stitch lines from either side of the snout up towards the ears in a circular shape to accentuate the shape of the face. Continue to make some random stitches onto the surface of the head and tail to give a little texture. A fluffy yarn could make a good alternative and make the wolf's features look really furry.

Skill level: ★★

Size
21.5cm (8½in) tall

You will need
- DK (light worsted) yarn:
  30g (1oz) each of olive green (A) and
  dark brown (B)
  20g (¾oz) each of flesh tone or taupe
  (C) and beige (D)
  Small amount of grey (E)
- 3mm (US D/3) crochet hook
- Removable stitch marker
- Tapestry needle
- Toy stuffing
- Black and red embroidery thread or
  2ply yarn
- 1 x 12cm (⅜ x 4¾in) piece of
  brown felt
- Small neutral coloured button
- Medium gauge wire – one 7.5cm (3in)
  length

Abbreviations

ch	chain
cont	continue
dc	double crochet
dc2tog	double crochet two sts together
htr	half treble
pm	place marker
rem	remaining
rep	repeat
ss	slip stitch
st(s)	stitch(es)
t-ch	turning chain
tr	treble
yrh	yarn round hook

BORIS THE WOODCUTTER

Boris saves the day, arriving just in time to frighten Mr Wolf away with his mighty axe.
(I prefer to think of Mr Wolf running off to live happily in the woods and vowing
never to be too greedy again!) Boris's body is worked in one piece, his boots are then
worked separately and stitched on at the end. His axe is simply made in wire using the
yarn wrapping technique, with the axe head worked into the end using double and
treble crochet.

HEAD AND BODY
Base ring: Using yarn C, 5ch, ss in first ch to join.
Round 1: 3ch (counts as 1tr now and
throughout), 11tr in ring, ss in 3rd ch of t-ch to
join. (12 sts)
Round 2: 3ch, [2tr in next st, 1tr] 5 times, 2tr in
last st, ss in 3rd ch of t-ch to join. (18 sts)
Rounds 3–12: Pm and (work in a spiral), dc
around. (18 sts)

Neck:
Round 13: [Dc2tog] 9 times. (9 sts)
Round 14: Dc around. (9 sts)
Fasten off yarn C, leaving a 7.5cm (3in) tail.
Round 15: Attach yarn D, dc around. (9 sts)
Fill head with toy stuffing.

Shoulders:
Work in rounds as follows:
Round 16: 3ch, 1tr in base of ch, 2tr in each st
around, ss in 3rd ch of t-ch to join. (18 sts)
Round 17: 3ch, [2tr in next st, 1tr] 8 times, 2tr in
last st, ss in 3rd ch of t-ch to join. (27 sts)

Armholes:
Round 18: 1ch, 4dc, miss 5 sts, 9dc, miss 5 sts,
4dc, ss in first dc to join (makes two armholes of
5 sts each and a body of 17 sts). Work into the
central 17 sts only in a spiral as follows:
Rounds 19–24: Pm, dc around. (17 sts)
Fasten off yarn C, leaving a 7.5cm (3in) tail.
Fill body with toy stuffing.

Trousers:

Rounds 25–28: Attach yarn D, pm, dc around. (17 sts)

Trouser legs:

Round 29: Insert hook into next st, miss next 8 sts, insert hook into next st, yrh, draw yarn through both sts leaving 1 loop on hook, cont to work 1dc into each st of first trouser leg. (8 sts) You should now have two leg-holes of 8 sts each.
Leg rounds 1–8: Pm in first st of first Leg round, dc around.
Fasten off yarn D, leaving a 7.5cm (3in) tail.
Re-attach yarn D at other leg-hole and rep.
Fasten off and weave in ends.
Fill legs with toy stuffing.

Arms:

Each arm is worked separately.
Attach yarn D at armpit join, 2dc in join, pm, dc around. (7 sts)
As you work arm put small amounts of stuffing into arm as you go.
Arm rounds 1–10: Dc around. (7 sts)
Fasten off yarn D, leaving a 7.5cm (3in) tail.

Hands:

Arm round 11: Attach yarn C, dc around. (7 sts)
Arm round 12: 1dc, [dc2tog] 3 times. (4 sts)
Fasten off and weave in all ends.
Rep for other arm.

BOOTS

(make 2)

Work in a spiral.

Base ring: Using yarn B, 2ch, 6dc in 2nd ch from hook, ss in first dc to join. (6 sts)

Round 1: Pm, dc around.

Round 2: [1dc, 2dc in next st] 3 times. (9 sts)

Rounds 3–5: Dc around.

Heel:

Round 7: 1ch, 4dc, turn, leaving rem 5 sts unworked. Work in rows as follows:

Rows 1–4: 1ch, 4dc, turn.

Row 5: 1ch, 4dc, do not turn but cont to work 1dc into rem 5 sts of Round 7.

Resume working in a spiral as before.

Rounds 6–11: Dc around.

At end of Round 11, ss in first dc to join.

Fasten off yarn B, leaving a 7.5cm (3in) tail.

HAT

Work in the round.

Base ring: Using yarn A, 5ch, ss in first ch to join.

Round 1: 3ch, 11tr in ring, ss in 3rd ch of t-ch to join. (12 sts)

Round 2: 3ch, [2tr in next st, 1tr] 5 times, 2tr in last st, ss in 3rd ch of t-ch to join. (18 sts)

Round 3: 3ch, tr around, ss in 3rd ch of t-ch to join. (18 sts)

Brim:

Round 4: 3ch, 1tr in base of ch, 2tr in each st around, ss in 3rd ch of t-ch to join. (36 sts)

Fasten off yarn A, leaving a 7.5cm (3in) tail.

HAIR

Row 1: Using yarn B, 14ch, 1dc in 2nd ch from hook, 1dc in each ch to end, turn. (13 sts)

Rows 2–3: 3ch, tr across, turn. (13 sts)

Fasten off yarn B, leaving a 15cm (6in) tail.

BEARD

Row 1: Using yarn B, 10ch, 1htr in 2nd ch from hook, 1htr in each ch to end. (8 sts)

Fasten off yarn B, leaving a 15cm (6in) tail.

FINISHING

Using tails and tapestry needle, stitch hat to the top of head, hair to the back of head under brim of hat, beard to chin (stitching ends of beard into sides of hair).

Fill each boot with toy stuffing. Using tapestry needle and tails of yarn B, sew a boot to the end of each leg.

Embroidery:

See pages 122–123 for details of embroidery stitches and page 124 for instructions on making a face. Use black embroidery thread to make two French knots for eyes.

Using yarn C, make a large French knot for a nose. Wrap yarn around French knot and stitch through to give it a bulbous shape.

Make two short straight sts for a mouth and three vertical sts in yarn B under his nose for a moustache.

Belt:

Wrap strip of brown felt around the waist and stitch in place.

Use black embroidery to attach button to the centre front as a buckle.

Head of axe:

Make the axe handle (see box, right)

Slip the crochet hook into the last cross stitch and using yarn E, join with a slip stitch (see diagram 1)

Row 1: 3ch (counts as 1tr), 3tr in joining ss, turn. 1ch, dc in each tr across, dc in 3rd ch of t-ch. Fasten off yarn E, using end to weave into axe to form shape and secure to axe handle (see diagram 2) You can spray a little stiffener onto the grey axe head to make it more rigid.

MAKING THE AXE HANDLE

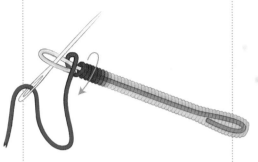

With the 7.5cm (3in) length of wire, bend a small loop at each end. Using a tapestry needle and length of yarn B, stitch around and through loop and wrap around wire to other end, continue until wire is fully covered and looks sturdy.

With yarn D and a tapestry needle, make a few cross stitches around the yarn wrapped wire.

1.

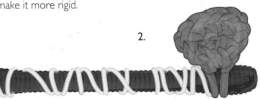

2.

RAPUNZEL

Rapunzel has a wired body so that she can be moved into different positions and is mostly worked in double crochet in a spiral using stitch markers. She has a high-waisted dress with a scalloped skirt and her long plait trails down her back and across the floor, but she can loop it over her arms. Her headdress is embroidered with flowers and leaves and finished with a pretty button.

Skill level: ★★★

Size
16.5cm (6½in) tall

You will need
- DK (light worsted) yarn:
  20g (¾oz) each of golden yellow (A) and flesh tone (B)
  30g (1oz) of pale pink (C)
  10g (⅜oz) of burgundy (D)
  Oddments of lime green (E)
- 3mm (US D/3) crochet hook
- Removable stitch marker
- Tapestry needle
- Toy stuffing
- Medium gauge wire – one 15cm (6in) length; one 20cm (8in) length; plus one 15cm (6in) length (optional)
- Black embroidery thread or 2ply yarn
- Button, 1cm (⅜in) diameter

Abbreviations
blo	back loop only
ch	chain
dc	double crochet
dc2tog	double crochet two sts together
pm	place marker
rem	remaining
rep	repeat
ss	slip stitch
st(s)	stitch(es)
t-ch	turning chain
tr	treble
tr2tog	treble crochet two sts together
yrh	yarn round hook

Special abbreviation
3tr cluster – *yrh, insert hook in the required stitch, yrh again and draw a loop through. Yrh, draw through 2 of the loops, leaving 2 loops on hook; rep from * twice more ending with 4 loops on hook, yrh and draw through all the loops on the hook to complete cluster.

HEAD AND BODY
Work from top of head down as follows:

Round 1: Using yarn B, 2ch, 9dc in 2nd ch from hook, ss in first dc to join. (9 sts)

Round 2: Pm, work in a spiral , 2dc in each st around. (18 sts)

Rounds 3–7: Dc around. (18 sts)

Fill head with toy stuffing.

Neck:
Round 8: [Dc2tog] 9 times. (9 sts)

Round 9: Dc around.

Shoulders:
Round 10: 1dc, 2dc in each of next 4 sts, 1dc, 2dc in each of next 3 sts. (16 sts)

Round 11: [2dc in next st, 1dc] 8 times. (24 sts)

Fasten off yarn B.

Dress:
Round 12: Join yarn C at st marker, dc around. (24 sts)

Armholes:
Round 13: 4dc, miss 4 sts, 8dc, miss 4 sts, 4dc (makes two armholes of 4 sts and a body of 6 sts). Work in rounds in central 16 sts only as follows:

Round 14: 3ch (counts as 1tr now and throughout), tr around, ss in 3rd ch of t-ch to join. (16 sts)

Fill upper body with toy stuffing.

Skirt:
Round 15: 1ch, *1dc, miss 1 st, 5tr in next st, miss 1 st; rep from * 3 more times, ss in first dc to join. (4 scallops)

Round 16: 3ch, 4tr in base of ch, 1dc in centre (3rd) tr of 5tr scallop *5tr in next dc, 1dc in centre (3rd) tr of 5tr scallop; rep from * 3 more times, ss to 3rd ch of t-ch to join. (5 scallops)

Rounds 17– 22: Rep Round 16, making sure each scallop is made in each dc of previous round.

Fasten off.

Edging:
Round 23: Join yarn E in blo at st marker, 3ch, 1tr(blo) at base of ch, 2tr(blo) in each st around, ss in 3rd ch of t-ch to join. (58 sts)

Fasten off.

Sleeves:
Work round each armhole separately.

Join yarn C at armpit, 2dc in join, pm, 1dc, 2dc in next st, 1dc. (6 sts)

Sleeve rounds 1–4: Dc around.

Frill:

Sleeve round 5: 3ch, 1tr in base of ch, 2tr in each st around, ss in 3rd ch of t-ch to join. (12 sts)

SKIRT BASE

Base ring: Using yarn E, 5ch, ss in first ch to join.
Round 1: 3ch, 11tr in ring, ss in 3rd ch of t-ch to join. (12 sts)
Round 2: 3ch, 1tr in base of ch, 2tr in each st around, ss in 3rd ch of t-ch to join. (24 sts)
Round 3: 3ch, 1tr in base of ch, 1tr, *2tr in next st, 1tr; rep from * around, ss in 3rd ch of t-ch to join. (36 sts)
Fasten off.

ARMS

Using the 15cm (6in) length of wire, follow the instructions in step 3 on page 125, using yarn B to wrap the hands and arms.

LEGS

Using the 20cm (8in) length of wire in half, follow the instructions in steps 4 and 5 on page 125. Insert the legs through the skirt base and push

the body and legs up inside the skirt. Add some toy stuffing around the legs and fill the skirt with more stuffing. Use the tail of yarn E to stitch the base up inside the skirt, so the ends of the wire legs protrude. Bend the ends of the wire legs into loops at each end to make feet.

Use yarn B to wrap the foot loop and legs. Stitch up through base of skirt and exit the needle near to the other wire leg, rep for the second leg working down towards foot. Stitch through loop several times to secure the yarn. Using a little of yarn C, stitch through each foot and wrap and stitch to cover the feet to make pink shoes.

HAIR

Base ring: Using yarn A, 2ch, 9dc in 2nd ch from hook, ss in first dc to join. (9 sts)
Round 1: 3ch, 1tr in base of ch, 2tr in each st around, ss in 3rd ch of t-ch to join. (18 sts)
Round 2: 3ch, 9tr, turn and work in rows (leaving rem 9 sts unworked) as follows:
Row 1: 3ch, tr across, turn. (9 sts).
Ss in next 4 sts, ready to work the plait in 5th st, leaving rem 4 sts unworked.

Plait:

Row 2: 1ch, make 3tr cluster in base of ch, turn.
Important note: There is no turning chain here, as this helps keep the 'plaits' more plump and defined.
Rows 3–30: 1ch, 3tr cluster in top of previous cluster, turn.
Fasten off A, leaving a long tail. Wrap tail 5 times around two fingers, insert hook through the 5 loops made, wrap yarn round hook and draw yarn through the loops to make a knot, making a small tassel. Trim the ends and separate the strands to look like hair.

FINISHING

Using yarn A, stitch hair to top of head with plait at centre back.
Bend arms and legs into desired position.

Embroidery:

See pages 122–123 for details of embroidery stitches and page 124 for instructions on making a face. Use black embroidery thread to embroider the eyes. Use a tiny scrap of yarn E to stitch a mouth.

Headdress:

Using green yarn, embroider some chain stitch leaves and with pink yarn, make French knots as flowers around the head and stitch a pretty button onto hair near the flowers.

Stand:

(optional)
Using 15cm (6in) length of wire, bend a loop over like a foot at one end and make a small hook at the other end.
Insert the hooked end up into the base under the skirt and pull back to catch the hook in the stuffing inside the dress.
Position to make sure that the figure stands up.
Using yarn E, stitch in and out of the base and wrap round wire support in the same way that you wrapped the arms and legs.
Bend the end of the stand with the loop into a right angle to make a concealed extra foot, stand Rapunzel upright and position as desired, the extra support will be concealed by the dress.

Skill level: ★★

Size

30cm (12in) tall (without roof)
39cm (15½in) tall (with roof)

You will need

- DK (light worsted) yarn:
  30g (1oz) of dark grey (A)
  100g (3½oz) of light grey (B)
  10g (⅜oz) of green (C)
  Tiny amount of yellow (D)
- 3mm (US D/3) crochet
  hook
- Removable stitch marker
- Tapestry needle
- Small amount of
  black felt
- Embroidery
  thread or 2ply
  yarn in black,
  pink and
  white
- Buttons – two
  5mm (¼in)
  diameter; three
  small buttons (for
  decoration only)
- Elastic – two 5cm
  (2in) pieces
- Fabric stiffener
  spray/spray
  starch or lining
  fabric (optional)
- PVA glue
  (optional)
- 30cm (12in)
  square of fabric
  for lining

See next page for
Abbreviations and
Special abbreviations

RAPUNZEL'S TOWER

There can be no finer way to store your knitting needles than in this quaint 'Rapunzel Tower', complete with golden hair falling from the tiny window at the top. Worked in the round using a basketweave stitch to simulate the stone construction, it can also easily be worked in plain double crochet or treble crochet, if you prefer. To make a shorter version, simply reduce the amount of rounds in your tower to your chosen height. A shorter tower makes a perfect home for crochet hooks!

BASE

With yarn A, 5ch, ss into first ch to make a ring.

Round 1: 1ch (doesn't count as a st now and throughout), 8dc in ring, ss into first dc to join. Place marker. (8 sts)

Round 2: 1ch, 2dc in each st around, ss to first dc to join. Move marker. (16 sts)

Round 3: 3ch (counts as 1 tr now and throughout), 2tr in each st round, ss into 3rd ch to join round. Remove marker and put aside. (32 sts)

Round 4: 3ch, 1tr in base of 3-ch, *1tr in next st, 2tr in next st; rep from * to last st, 1 tr in last st, ss into 3rd ch of t-ch to join. (48 sts)

Round 5: 1ch, 1dc into each st across, ss into first dc to join.

Fasten off yarn A, leaving a 7.5cm (3in) long tail.

Walls:

Round 6: Attach yarn B to end of Round 5. Work 1ch, place marker then 1dc(blo) into each st across, ss into first dc to join. (48 sts)

Round 7: 1ch, 1dc into next 3 sts, *dc2tog, 1dc into each of next 6 sts; rep from * 5 more times, dc2tog, 1dc into next 3 sts. (42 sts)

Round 8: Work Base ring of BW patt (see page 98).

Rounds 9–20: Work Rounds 1 and 2 of BW patt, ending after a Round 2.

Important: After each following decrease, keep continuity of patt to end of each round.

Round 21: 3ch, tr2tog, work BW patt to end of round, ss in 3rd ch of t-ch to join. (41 sts)

Rounds 22–26: 3ch, work BW patt to end of round, ss in 3rd ch of t-ch to join. (41 sts)

Round 27: 3ch, tr2tog, work BW patt to end, ss in 3rd ch of t-ch to join. (40 sts)

Round 28: 3ch, *tr2tog, work BW patt for 18 sts; rep from *, ss in 3rd ch of t-ch to join. (38 sts)

Round 29: 3ch, *tr2tog, work BW patt for 17 sts; rep from *, ss in 3rd ch of t-ch to join. (36 sts)

Round 30: 3ch, *tr2tog, work BW patt for 16 sts; rep from *, ss in 3rd ch of t-ch to join. (34 sts)

Window ledge:

Round 31: Working in front loops only, 1ch, 1dc(flo) in next st, *1dc(flo) in next st, 2dc(flo) in next st, 1dc(flo) in next st; rep from * 11 times, ss in first dc to join. (45 sts)

Round 32: Working into back loops of Round 30 only, 2ch (counts as 1 htr now and throughout), 1htr in each st around, ss into 2nd ch of t-ch to join. (34 sts)

Round 33: 2ch, 1htr in each st around, ss in 2nd ch of t-ch to join. (34 sts)

Round 34: Rep Round 33. (34 sts)

Important: After each following increase, keep continuity of patt to end of each round as before.

Round 35: 2ch, 2htr in next st, 1htr in each of next 16 sts, 2htr in next st, 1 htr in each st to end, ss in 2nd ch of t-ch to join. (36 sts)

Round 36: 2ch, 1htr each st around, ss in 2nd ch of t-ch to join. (36 sts)

Fasten off yarn B, leaving a 20cm (8in) tail.

Abbreviations

blo	back loop only
ch	chain
dc	double crochet
flo	front loop only
htr	half treble
patt	pattern
rep	repeat
ss	slip stitch
t-ch	turning chain
tr	treble
tr2tog	treble two sts together
yrh	yarn round hook

Special abbreviations

Raised treble front (RtrF) – yrh, insert hook behind stem of required stitch (from front to back, right to left), yrh, pull up a loop, yrh, pull through two loops (2 loops on hook), yrh, pull through remaining two loops to complete the stitch.

Raised treble back (RtrB) – yrh, insert hook behind stem of required stitch (from back to front, right to left), yrh, pull up a loop, yrh, pull through two loops (2 loops on hook), yrh, pull through remaining two loops to complete the stitch.

Basketweave stitch (BW patt) – work in the round, without turning and keeping RS facing you, as follows:
Base ring: 3ch (counts as 1 tr now and throughout), 1tr into each st across, ss into 3rd ch of t-ch to join.
Round 1: 3ch, 1RtrF in next st, *1RtrB in next st, 1RtrF in next st; rep from * to end, ss into 3rd ch of t-ch to join.
Round 2: 3ch, 1RtrB into next st, *1RtrF into next st, 1RtrB into next st; rep from * to end, ss into 3rd ch of t-ch to join.
Rep Rounds 2 and 3 as instructed in patt.

Grass:

Attach yarn C to the front loop of any st in Round 5.
Working in the flo, 1ch, 1dc(flo) in each st to end of round, ss into first dc to join. (48 sts)
Next round: 1ch, *1dc into next 3 sts, 1htr, 1tr, 1htr; rep from * 8 times.
Fasten off yarn C, leaving a long tail. Use long tail to stitch each tr to wall of tower to make a point. (8 points around tower)

ROOF

(Worked from top down)
Base ring: Using yarn A, 2ch, 6dc into second ch from hook, ss in first dc to join round. (6 sts)
Place st marker in first st and continue in spirals, moving the st marker at the end of every round.
Rounds 1–3: 1dc in each st around. (6 sts)
Round 4: *1dc, 2dc in next st; rep from * 3 times. (9 sts)
Rounds 5–7: 1dc in each st around. (9 sts)
Round 8: *2dc, 2dc in next st; rep 3 times. (12 sts)
Round 9: *2dc in next st, 5dc; rep from *. (14 sts)
Round 10: 2dc in first st, *2dc in next st, 1dc in next st, 2dc in next st; rep from * 4 times, 2dc into last st. (24 sts)
Round 11: 1dc in each st around.
Round 12: Rep Round 11. (24 sts)
Round 13: 2dc in first st, 1dc in each st to end of round. (25 sts)
Round 14: *1dc, 2dc in next st, 1dc, 2dc in next st, 1dc; rep from * 4 more times. (35 sts)
Round 15: 1dc in each st around.
Round 16: 2dc in first st, 1dc in each st around. (36 sts)
Round 17: *2dc, 2dc in next st; rep from * 11 more times. (48 sts)

Rounds 18–20: 1dc in each st around, ss in first dc to join.
Fasten off yarn A, leaving a 7.5cm (3in) tail.

FINISHING

Stitch on a couple of buttons to decorate the roof and near the grass at foot of tower.

Windows:

Stitch 3 felt window shapes (see photograph) above window ledge (Round 31) with the larger shape in the centre and the narrower shapes at each side.
With white embroidery thread or 2 ply yarn, make a cross stitch through each window shape to look like leaded glass.

Rapunzel's plait:

Using a small amount of yellow yarn (held double), 52ch, fasten off yarn and trim ends about 1.5cm (⅝in) from end of ch.
With tapestry needle, stitch other end of ch to bottom of centre window, leaving chain plait hanging down.

Stiffening:

Place a cardboard tube or rolling pin into tower and spray fabric stiffener on the surface, leave to dry for 24 hours.
Rep with roof section, filling it with a little newspaper to keep it in shape.

Fastenings:

Stitch a small button to the inside of the top of the tower on each side – you can leave one button fastened and use the other to open and close your case.
Make a fabric lining (see box, opposite).

"Rapunzel, Rapunzel,
let down your hair"

RAPUNZEL'S TOWER LINING

Cut a piece of fabric 21 x 30cm (8½ x 12in). Turn a hem to the wrong side on one short end. Fold the fabric in half lengthways right sides together and sew down the length with a 1cm (⅜in) seam allowance to make a tube.

Cut a 9cm (3½in) diameter circle of fabric. Hand sew running stitch around the edge of the circle and gently gather to fit inside the base of the tube.

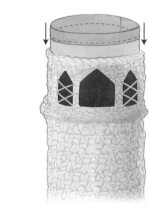

Stitch the gathered circle inside the tube with right sides together, easing where necessary.

Slide the tube of fabric inside the tube of crochet and slipstitch to the inside of the crochet edge. On either side of the tower on the inside stitch a small button.

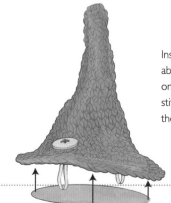

Inside the roof stitch two small loops of narrow elastic, each about 2cm (¾in) long, to match the position of the buttons on the tower. Cut a 5cm (2in) diameter circle of felt and stitch inside the bottom of the roof to hide the raw ends of the elastic button loops.

Tip
For a frosted effect you can add a little PVA glue onto the roof and sprinkle silver glitter onto the glue, shaking off any excess.

Size

20cm (8in) tall (including crown)

You will need

- DK (light worsted) yarn:
  10g (⅜oz) of dark brown (A)
  20g (¾oz) each of flesh tone (B), green
  (C), blue (D), red (E) and white (F)
  10g (⅜oz) each of black (G) and
  gold metallic
  Small amount of silver
- 6 small gold beads
- 3mm (US D/3) crochet hook
- Removable stitch marker
- Tapestry needle
- Toy stuffing
- Embroidery thread – black, red
  and beige
- Sewing needle
- Pointed end of a bamboo skewer cut
  to about 8cm (3¼in) long (use wire if
  you prefer)
- Household match with the end cut off
- Black permanent marker pen or a little
  black or silver paint/silver nail polish
- Double-sided sticky tape

Abbreviations

ch	chain
cont	continue
dc	double crochet
dc2tog	double crochet two sts together
flo	front loop only
htr	half treble
pm	place marker
rep	repeat
ss	slip stitch
st(s)	stitch(es)
t-ch	turning chain
tr	treble

Special abbreviation

3ch picot – 3ch, ss in 3rd ch from hook.

RAPUNZEL'S PRINCE

The Prince is made using double, half treble and treble crochet. In order to make the Prince a little more stable, I have worked the boots separately and then stitched them to the legs at the end. The figure does not need wiring inside but you could wire the arms and legs if you like, following the instructions on page 125. To make him suitable for younger children, use French knots instead of beads on his tunic.

BODY AND HEAD

Base ring: Using yarn B, 2ch, 8dc in 2nd ch from hook, ss in first dc to join. (8 sts)
Round 1: Pm, 2dc in each st around. (16 sts)
Round 2: [2dc in next st, 7dc into each of next 7 sts] twice. (18 sts)
Rounds 3–9: Dc around. (18 sts)
Round 10: [Dc2tog] 9 times. (9 sts)
Round 11: Dc around. (9 sts)
Fasten off yarn B, leaving a 7.5cm (3in) tail.
Fill head with toy stuffing.

Shoulders:

Round 12: Join yarn C at st marker, 3ch, 1tr in base of ch, 2tr in each st around. (18 sts)
Round 13: Dc around.
Round 14: [2dc in next st, 2dc] 6 times. (24 sts)

Armholes:

Round 15: 3dc, miss 6 sts, 6dc, miss 6 sts, 3dc (makes 2 armholes of 6 sts each and a body of 12 sts).

Tunic:

Work around the centre 12 sts in rounds using t-chs as follows:
Rounds 16–17: Pm, dc around. (12 sts)
Round 18: 3ch, 1tr in base of ch, 2tr in each st around, ss in 3rd ch of t-ch to join round. (24 sts)
Round 19: 2ch (counts as 1htr now and throughout), htr around. (24 sts)
Fasten off yarn C, leaving a 7.5cm (3in) tail.
Fill body with toy stuffing.

Breeches:

Work from centre back of figure in a spiral.
Round 20: Join yarn D at centre back of WS (under hem of tunic) of Round 18, pm, dc(flo) around. (24 sts)
Round 21: Insert hook into next st, miss 11 sts, insert hook into next st, yrh, draw yarn through both st (makes two legs of 11 sts each).
Set up the first leg as follows: 1dc, pm, 10dc. (11 sts)

Leg rounds 1–6: Dc around.

Fasten off yarn D, leaving a 7.5cm (3in) tail.

Re-attach yarn D to other leg-hole and rep for second leg.

Fill breeches with toy stuffing.

Arms:

Work in a spiral. Attach yarn F at armpit join, 2dc in join, pm, 8dc. (8 sts)

Fill arm with toy stuffing every couple of rounds.

Rounds 1–5: Dc around.

Round 6: Dc2tog, 6dc. (7 sts)

Round 7: Dc2tog, 5dc. (6 sts)

Round 8: Dc2tog, 4dc. (5 sts)

Fasten off yarn F, leaving a 7.5cm (3in) tail.

Round 9: Attach yarn B at st marker, dc around.

Fasten off yarn B, leaving a long tail. Use tail to stitch through last round, drawing sts into a hand shape. Weave in end.

Re-attach yarn F and rep for the other arm.

BOOTS

(make 2)

Base ring: Using yarn G, 2ch, 6dc in 2nd ch from hook, ss in first dc to join. (6 sts)

Rounds 1–2: Pm, dc around.

Round 3: [2dc in next st, 2dc] twice. (8 sts)

Heel:

Round 4: 3ch, 1tr at base of ch, 2tr in each of next 3 sts, 3dc. (12 sts)

Rounds 5–12: Dc around. (12 sts)

Fasten off yarn G, leaving a 12.5cm (5in) tail.

Fill each boot with toy stuffing. Use tapestry needle and tail of G to stitch the boots to the ends of the breeches.

The legs are not wired so the figure will not be able to stand up unaided.

SWORD

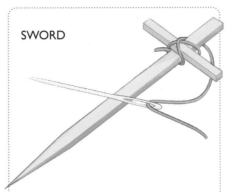

Put the bamboo skewer and matchstick together in a cross shape with the longer piece extending at the bottom. Use a length of any yarn to wrap tightly around the part where the two pieces cross. Stitch around several times to secure.

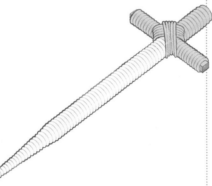

Wrap a little double-sided sticky tape around the point of the sword and proceed to wrap the silver yarn around towards the hilt. You can use a plain grey yarn on the top end to look like steel. It can be difficult to wrap right up to the ends so leave a tiny gap and fill in the ends with your marker, paint or, as in my case, metallic nail polish.

HAIR

Base ring: Using yarn A, 2ch, 8dc in 2nd ch from hook, ss in first dc to join. (8 sts)

Round 1: Pm, 3ch, 1tr in base of ch, 2tr in each st around, ss in 3rd ch of t-ch to join. (16 sts)

Round 2: Dc around.

Round 3: 3ch, 10tr, turn, leaving rem 5 sts unworked.

Cont in a row as follows:

Row 1: 3ch, tr across. (12 sts)

Fasten off yarn A, leaving a 7.5cm (3in) tail.

CROWN

Row 1: Using gold yarn, 20ch, 1tr in 4th ch from hook, 1tr in each ch. (18 sts)

Row 2: 1ch, ss in 1st tr [ch3, ss in same st, ss into next 3 sts] rep 6 times. (7 picots)

Fasten off gold yarn, leaving a 12.5cm (5in) tail.

Stitch ends of crown together into a ring.

CLOAK

Row 1: Using yarn E, 19ch, 1dc in 2nd ch from hook, dc in each ch across. (18 sts)

Rows 2–6: 3ch, tr across.

Fasten off yarn E. Weave in ends.

Neck ruffle:

Using yarn E, 3ch, yrh, 3tr in 3rd ch from hook.

Fasten off, leaving a 7.5cm (3in) tail.

FINISHING

Belt:

Using a length of yarn A, 25ch, ss in 5th ch from hook to make a loop. 20ch, ss in first ch made and fasten off. Weave in ends.

Place the belt diagonally over the Prince's shoulder, under the cape and with the loop sitting on his hip. Insert finished sword into loop.

Using end of gold yarn and tapestry needle, stitch crown to the top of the head.

Stitch 6 gold beads down the front of the tunic.

Stitch cloak to the shoulders of prince with the gold yarn used for the crown.

Stitch neck ruffle under chin using tail of yarn E.

Skill level: ★

Size

12.5cm (5in) tall (including chimney)

You will need

- DK (light worsted) yarn:
  25g (⅞oz) each in three contrasting shades
- 3mm (US D/3) crochet hook
- Small scraps of felt or fabric
- Small amounts of embroidery thread or 2ply yarn in different colours
- Removable stitch marker
- Pretty buttons (optional)
- Bead and twine (optional)
- Toy stuffing

Abbreviations

blo	back loop only
ch	chain
ch sp	chain space
dc	double crochet
dtr	double treble
rep	repeat
ss	slip stitch
st(s)	stitch(es)
t-ch	turning chain
WS	wrong side

TOADSTOOL HOUSE

Your toadstool should stand up neatly, but if you wish you can attach a loop to the centre of the roof in place of the chimney so that you can hang it up – attach the loop through the cap before assembling the pieces. They look charming as Christmas tree decorations, especially if you make several in different bright colours.

STALK AND GILLS

Base:

Using first colour, 5ch, join with ss in 5th ch from hook to make ring, 1ch, 10dc in ring, ss to first dc to join. Place st marker to show end of round. Move the marker up each round worked.
(10 sts)

Round 1: 1ch, 2dc in each st to end. (20 sts)

Round 2: 1ch, turn to WS, ss in back loop only of next st, 1dc(blo) around, ss to first dc to join.
(20 sts)

Stalk:

Rounds 3–8: Dc around, working in a spiral – no t-ch at the beginning of each round. (20 sts)

Round 7: *1ch, miss next st, 1dc; rep from * to end of round. (10 sts + 10 ch sps)

Round 8: 1ch, 1dc in each ch sp, ss to first dc to join. (10 sts)

Rounds 9–12: 1ch, dc around. (10 sts)

Fasten off first colour.

Gills:

Change to second colour.

Round 13: 4ch, 1dtr in base of ch, 2dtr in each st to end, ss to 4th ch of t-ch join. (20 sts)

Rounds 14–15: 1ch, dc around, ss to first dc to join. (20 sts)

Fasten off second colour, leaving a 30cm (12in) long tail.

CAP

Using third colour, 5ch, join with ss to 5th ch from hook.

Round 1: 1ch, 10dc in ring, ss in first dc to join. Place st marker.

Round 2: 1ch, 2dc in each st to end, ss in first dc to join. (20 sts)

Round 3: Rep Round 2. (40 sts)

Rounds 4–8: Dc around, working in a spiral. Finish last round with a ss in first dc of previous round.

Fasten off third colour.

FINISHING

Fill Stalk firmly with stuffing (should be free standing).

Using contrasting thread, work French knots (see page 122) at random over Cap.

Cut squares and rectangles of felt or fabric in different colours, place on Stalk and Cap to represent door and windows, then neatly backstitch in place.

Chimney:

Cut a piece of felt about 2.5 x 5cm (1 x 2in) and roll up into a tube. Stitch or glue neatly in place then attach to Cap by stitching down through tube into centre of Cap and sewing securely on the underside.

Put a little stuffing into Cap and then place Stalk and gills up inside. Using yarn end on gills, backstitch inside of Cap to gills.

Skill level: ★ / ★★

Size

Circle: 10cm (4in) diameter
Toadstools: From 2.5cm (1in) to 6.5cm
(2½in)

You will need

- DK (light worsted) yarn
  25g (⅞oz) each of red (A), beige (B),
  three shades of green (C, D and E)
  and cream (F)
- 3mm (US D/3) crochet hook
- Removable stitch marker
- Medium gauge wire – approx 20cm
  (8in) cut into 5 different lengths
- Small pliers
- Tapestry needle
- PVA glue
- Felt – two 10cm (4in) diameter circles
  in green, brown or beige
- Toy stuffing
- Small amount of 2ply yarn in cream or
  white

Abbreviations

ch	chain
ch sp	chain space
dc	double crochet
rep	repeat
ss	slip stitch
st(s)	stitch(es)
t-ch	turning chain
tr	treble

FAIRY RING PINCUSHION

This enchanting little piece of whimsy is made in a round and then the wire wrapped toadstools are added. There is something very therapeutic about making the toadstools – I have made classic red and white ones as in traditional fairytales, but you can play around with different colour and pattern combinations and decorate as you choose.

TOADSTOOL CAP

(make 5 – 2 small and 3 large)
Round 1: Using yarn A, 2ch, 12tr in second ch from hook, ss into first tr to join. (12 sts)
Stop after Round 1 for the small Toadstools.
Continue to Round 2 for the large toadstools.
Round 2: 1ch, 1dc into each st around, ss in first dc to join.
Both toadstools: Fasten off.

Gills:

Using yarn B, 5ch, join with ss to make a ring.
1ch, 12dc in ring, ss in first dc to join.
Fasten off, leaving a long tail.

STALK

(make 5)
Push a small length of wire through centre of the Gills, bend end over on inside of gills to secure and stitch in place using cream or white yarn. Insert threaded tapestry needle back through centre of Gills near the wire and wrap tightly down the wire until fully covered. Stitch back and forth a few times through wire wrapping to secure and fasten off. Dip yarn ends into PVA glue to keep in place. Allow to dry fully. Repeat for all 5 stalks and set aside.

GRASS

Using yarn C, 5ch, ss into first ch to make a ring.
Round 1: 4ch (counts as 1tr, 1ch), *1tr in ring, 1ch; rep from * 7 more times, ss in 3rd ch of t-ch to join round. (9 sts)
Place st marker here and work in spiral from here onwards.
Round 2: *2tr in each ch sp, 2ch; rep from * to st marker. (18 sts)
Round 3: Move st marker, change to yarn D, rep Round 2. (18 sts)
Rounds 4–5: Move st marker, change to yarn E and work [2tr in each ch sp, 3ch] to end of round. (18 sts)
Round 6: Move st marker, change to yarn C, 1ch, *3dc into next ch sp, 1ch; rep from * to end of round, ss in first dc to join.
Fasten off yarn C.
Weave in all ends.
The fabric will curve into a domed shape – stretch and gently block to flatten shape slightly.

FINISHING

Place stalk and gills up into Toadstool caps and stitch neatly in place around the edge using yarn B. Using cream yarn, make random small stitches on cap to look like toadstool spots, or sew on tiny beads or sequins.

Rep for all toadstools.

Stitch the crochet dome shape onto one circle of felt.

Arrange toadstools in circular shape and when you are happy with the position, push the wire end of each toadstool down through the right side of crochet and felt circle, bend ends over on the underside of felt circle, stitch in place with tapestry needle and a length of yarn C.

Stitch the other circle of felt to the other circle to make a base, using yarn D and neat blanket stitches about 2mm (⅛in) apart around circumference. Leave a little gap and fill shape with toy stuffing, close with blanket stitch and fasten off yarn D. Ensure the blanket stitch is sufficiently close to retain the stuffing.

Scallop edging:

Work sts into blanket stitches around circle as follows:

Using cream yarn, attach yarn to any blanket stitch around circle.

Work 1ch, *1dc in next blanket stitch, 2tr in next blanket stitch, 1dc in next blanket stitch, ss in next blanket stitch; rep from * around (approx 18 times), ss into first ch to join.

Fasten off, weaving in ends.

Skill level: ★★ / ★★★

Size

13cm (5¼in) tall

You will need

- DK (light worsted) yarn:
  25g (⅞oz) of white (A)
  35g (1oz) of dark green (B)
  20g (¾oz) each of dark brown (C)
  and light green (D)
- Medium gauge wire – 30cm (12in)
  length
- Small piece of air-drying clay to make
  base with 5cm (2in) circumference
- 5cm (2in) diameter green felt circle
- 3mm (US D/3) crochet hook
- Removable stitch marker
- Tapestry needle
- White sewing thread
- Sewing needle
- Selection of beads, sequins and trims
  to decorate (optional)

Abbreviations

blo	back loop only
ch	chain
dc	double crochet
pm	place marker
ss	slip stitch
st(s)	stitch(es)
WS	wrong side

Special abbreviations

5ch picot – 5ch, ss in 5th ch from hook.
7ch picot – 7ch, ss in 7th ch from hook.

SNOW CAPPED FIR TREES

These are quite addictive to make and once you understand the construction you can make a host of trees in varying heights to build your own frosted forest.
You can leave the trees plain or decorate as you wish. I have just stitched a few silver and white sequins on at the end but you could use colourful pompom edgings, ribbons and brightly coloured beads, sequins and buttons. Add a loop into inside top to make charming tree decorations.

TREE

The tree is made in 4 sections, worked from the top down.
Each section is worked in a spiral with a st marker at the beginning of the section. At the end of each section, fasten off yarn leaving a 7.5cm (3in) tail.
To work the next section, turn to WS, re-attach yarn and work into the back loops of the penultimate round (inside tree).
If you find it difficult to find the loops to work into, turn to WS, fold the work forwards at desired round, this will expose the horizontal bar at back of the st.

First section:

Base ring: With yarn A, 2ch, 6dc in 2nd ch from hook, ss in first dc to join.
Rounds 1–4: Pm, dc around. (6 sts)
Fasten off yarn A, leaving a 7.5cm (3in) tail.
Round 5: Attach yarn B, dc(blo) around. (6 sts)
Round 6: [2dc in next st, 1dc] 3 times. (9 sts)
Round 7: [2dc into next st, 2dc] 3 times. (12 sts)

Fir branches:

Work chain loop pattern as follows:
Round 8: *1dc, [5ch picot, 7ch picot, 5ch picot] in dc, 2dc; rep from * 3 times. (4 fir branches)
Fasten off yarn B, leaving a 7.5cm (3in) tail.

Second section:

Round 9: Rejoin Yarn B to blo of any WS st in Round 7, pm, dc around. (12 sts)
Round 10: Dc around. (12 sts)

Round 11: [1dc, 2dc in next st] 6 times. (18 sts)
Round 12: Dc around. (18 sts)

Fir branches:

Round 13: As Round 8, but work 6 fir branches.
Fasten off yarn B and re-attach in same way as before to Round 12.

Third section:

Round 14: Pm, dc(blo) around. (18 sts)
Round 15: Dc around. (18 sts)
Round 16: [2dc in next st, 2dc] 6 times. (24 sts)

Fir branches:

Round 17: As for Rounds 8 and 13 but work pattern 8 times to end of round.
Fasten off yarn B and re-attach in same way as before to Round 16.

Fourth section:

Round 18: Pm, dc(blo) around. (24 sts)
Round 19: Dc around. (24 sts)
Round 20: [2dc in next st, 3dc] 6 times. (30 sts)
Round 21: Dc around. (30 sts)

Fir Branches:

Round 23: As Rounds 8, 13 and 17 but work 10 fir branches.
Fasten off yarn B. Weave in all loose ends.

Snow trimmed edging:

Work edging around each of rounds 8, 13, 17 and 23.
Attach yarn A between two 5ch picots and work as follows:

Work around 1st 5ch picot, *ss into each of next 2 (outside loops of picot) ch, 3dc into 3rd of 5ch picot (at tip of picot), ss into (each outside loops of) next 2 ch*.

Work around next 7ch picot, ss into next 3 ch, 3dc into 4th of 7ch picot (at tip), ss into next 2 3-ch, rep from * to * around third 5ch picot, miss next ch and ss into each of 2dc between the two sets of fir branches

Rep the edging around each of fir branches to end of round.

Rep edging at Rounds 8, 13, 17 and 13 as above.

Fasten off yarn A and weave in all ends.

GRASS

Base ring: Using yarn D, ch5, ss into 1st ch to join a ring.

Round 1: Ch3, 10tr into ring, ss into 3rd ch to join round. (10 sts)

Round 2: Ch3, 2tr into each st to end of round, ss into 3rd ch to join round. (20 sts)

Round 3: Ch3, 2tr into each st to end of round. (40 sts)

Round 4: Ch1, 1dc into all sts to end of round, ss into ch to join round. (40 sts)

Fasten off yarn D and leave a 25cm (10in) end.

FINISHING

Trunk:
Using the 30cm (12in) length of wire, bend in half twisting each half around the other tightly. The trunk will now be 15cm (6in) long. Set aside.

Base:
Roll the piece of clay into a ball, press down onto a flat tray or plate and mould into a dome shape, stick wire trunk into the clay to a depth of about 1.5cm (⅝in) and remove, leaving a hole, leave clay to dry for 24 hours. Follow glue instructions for drying times.

When dry, insert wire through centre of crochet disc, and then put end of wire into hole in clay with a drop of glue to secure it. Ease crochet dome down over clay base.

Using long end of D and darning needle, stitch felt circle to crochet dome around and under clay base.

Using C, and darning needle, (with knot in end to secure) stitch through crochet base close to the wire trunk, wrap yarn around and along length of trunk until fully covered, stitching through yarn occasionally to keep yarn in place. Turn the tree inside out and stitch the end of the trunk to the top of the inside of the tree.

Turn tree right side out over trunk and tweak into position until the tree stands independently. To make the branches stick out, pull branches out and downwards and use spray starch or fabric stiffener on branches. Allow to dry. You can now stitch tiny sequins, beads and trimmings onto your tree.

Tip
If you prefer, you can stick sequins and decorations on with a little glue. If you dab a little glue to top of tree and edging around branches you can then sprinkle glitter onto them.

Skill level: ★★★

Size
26.5cm (10½in) long

You will need
- DK (light worsted) yarn:
  50g (1¾oz) of dark green (A)
  20g (¾oz) of light green (B)
- 3mm (US D/3) crochet hook
- Removable stitch marker
- Medium gauge wire – one 15cm (6in)
  length; one 20cm (8in) length
- 2 small diamond-shape pieces of red
  felt (or red/orange beads)
- 4 small pieces of dark green or
  brown felt
- Tapestry needle
- Embroidery thread or 2ply yarn in
  green
- Toy stuffing
- Removable stitch marker

Abbreviations
alt	alternate
ch	chain
ch sp	chain space
cont	continue
dc	double crochet
dc2tog	double crochet two sts together
dtr	double treble
htr	half treble
pm	place marker
rep	repeat
ss	slip stitch
st(s)	stitch(es)
tr	treble

SCARY DRAGON

The body of this dragon is worked in one piece in a spiral with stitch markers; the legs, spines, feet and other features are worked into the finished shape or added on after the body is complete. I have made my dragon a traditional green, but you could use red for a Welsh dragon or any other combination of colours.

BODY AND HEAD
The body is worked in one piece from the tail up. Fill the parts with toy stuffing as you work through the pattern to minimize over stuffing.

Tail:
Using yarn A, 2ch, 8dc in 2nd ch from hook, ss in first dc to join. (8 sts)

Rounds 1–10: Pm, 1ch, dc around, ss to first dc to join.

Round 11: 1ch, [2dc in next st, 3dc] twice, ss to first dc to join. (10 sts)

Rounds 12–16: Rep Round 1.

Round 17: 1ch, [2dc, 2dc in next st, 2dc] twice, ss to first dc to join. (12 sts)

Rounds 18–22: Rep Round 1.

Round 23: 1ch, [1dc, 2dc in next st] 6 times, ss to first dc to join. (18 sts)

Rounds 24–28: Rep Round 1.

Round 29: 1ch, 1dc, [2dc in next st, 3dc] 4 times, 1dc in last st, ss to first dc to join. (22 sts)

Round 30: 1ch, [2dc in next st, 10dc] twice, ss to first dc to join. (24 sts)

Rounds 31–40: Rep Round 1.

Round 41: Turn, 1ch, [1dc, dc2tog] 4 times, turn, 1ch, 8dc then cont to work 1dc in each st to end of round, ss to first dc to join. (20 sts)

Round 42: 1ch, 1dc, dc2tog, dc around, ss to first dc to join. (19 sts)

Round 43: 1ch, 6dc, [dc2tog] 4 times, dc to end, ss to first dc to join. (15 sts)

Neck:
Round 1: 1ch, [1dc, dc2tog] 5 times, ss to first dc to join. (10 sts)

Rounds 2–6: Rep Round 1.

Round 7: 1ch, [1dc, dc2tog, 2dc] twice, ss to first dc to join. (8 sts)

Rounds 8–10: 1ch, dc around, ss to first dc to join.

Shape head:
Round 11: 1ch, 1dc [1dc, dc2tog] twice, 1dc, ss to first dc to join. (6 sts)

Round 12: 1ch, 1dc, 2dc in next st, 2dc, 2dc in next st, 1dc, ss to first dc to join. (8 sts)

Round 13: 1ch, [1dc, 2dc in next st] 4 times. (12 sts)

Round 14: 1ch, 2dc in each st around. (24 sts)

Chin and snout:
Fold last round in half, giving you two sides of 12 sts each, making sure the fold lines up with chest shaping.

Ss through first and last 6 sts, joining the fabric, leaving rem 12 sts unworked (see diagram 1). Fill with stuffing.

Brow/forehead:
Next round: 1ch, [dc2tog] 6 times (shapes forehead, see diagram 2).

Fasten off, leaving a long tail. Use tail to weave through last round, tightening to close any holes.

2.

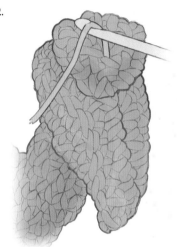

Spine:
Using yarn B and tapestry needle, embroider chain stitch (see page 122) along spine from top of head to tail.

As you work along spine, stitch dragon's head into a more upright position.

Spikes:
Attach yarn B to end of chain at top of head, 1dc in first chain stitch, *ch3, ss in 3rd ch from hook, 1dc in next chain stitch; rep from * along spine to end of tail.

Fasten off yarn B and weave in ends. The exact number of spikes does not matter as long as they correspond with the embroidered chain stitches.

Tail spade:
Using yarn B, 10ch, ss in first ch from hook, work in each ch across as follows: *1dc, 1htr, 3tr, 1htr, 1dc; 3ch, ss in base of ch, rep from * along other side of 8ch, ss in first ss to join.

Fasten off. Attach tail spade to end of tail.

1.

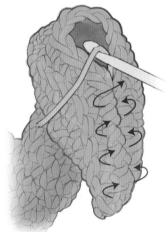

"The king's daughter had been carried off by a mighty dragon"

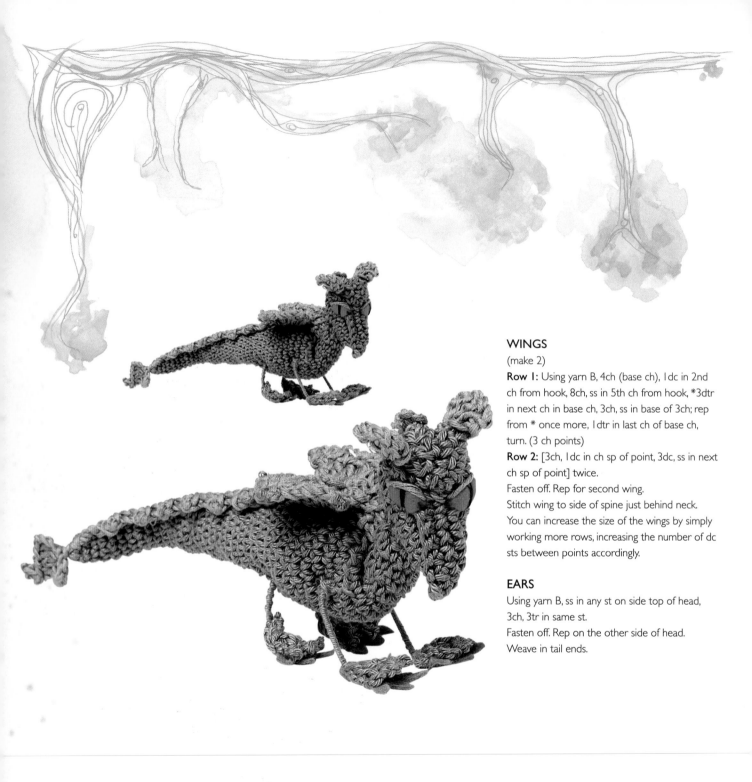

WINGS

(make 2)

Row 1: Using yarn B, 4ch (base ch), 1dc in 2nd ch from hook, 8ch, ss in 5th ch from hook, *3dtr in next ch in base ch, 3ch, ss in base of 3ch; rep from * once more, 1dtr in last ch of base ch, turn. (3 ch points)

Row 2: [3ch, 1dc in ch sp of point, 3dc, ss in next ch sp of point] twice.

Fasten off. Rep for second wing.

Stitch wing to side of spine just behind neck.

You can increase the size of the wings by simply working more rows, increasing the number of dc sts between points accordingly.

EARS

Using yarn B, ss in any st on side top of head, 3ch, 3tr in same st.

Fasten off. Rep on the other side of head.

Weave in tail ends.

LEGS

Using two 10cm (4in) lengths of wire, push each through belly area of body. Fold down on either side of body and curl each end into a loop for feet. Using yarn A, stitch legs in place by pushing needle through body and round wire (you may have to stitch quite a few times to make the wire stay in place). When legs feel secure, push needle and thread back through at top of wire and wrap yarn tightly around working downward to foot area. At loop end (foot), stitch round several times through loop covering all wire with yarn, leaving a length of yarn to attach feet. Rep until all four legs are covered with yarn.

FEET

(make 4)
Using yarn A, 2ch (base ch), ss in 2nd ch from hook, 6ch, 1tr in base ch, [3ch, 2tr in base ch] twice.
Fasten off.

FINISHING

Stitch Feet to top of wire loop feet. Cut four triangles of green or brown felt slightly larger than feet, cutting talon shapes at wide end. Stitch or glue to bottoms of the feet to cover wire.

Eyes:

Cut 2 small diamonds from red or orange felt and stitch on face either side of nose. Using black thread stitch a line through centre of each eye.

Wings:

Using yarn A, chain st from bottom of wing in straight lines to the end of each point.

Tips

When wrapping the legs, a little bit of double-sided sticky tape wrapped around the wire can help to keep the yarn securely attached.

Customize the shape to your own wishes, by adjusting the length of the legs, tail or wings, for example.

You could also cut a flame shaped piece of orange felt and stitch it to the dragon's mouth to make him into a fire-breathing dragon!

Skill level: ★★

Size

Cottage: 7.5 x 5 x 7.5cm (3 x 2 x 3in)
Garden: 10 x 12.5cm (4 x 5in)

You will need

Cottage:
- DK (light worsted) yarn:
  30g (1oz) of cream (A)
  10g (⅜oz) of light brown (B)
  Scrap of bright pink
- Black felt – four 1.5cm (⅝in) squares
- Blue felt – 1 x 2.5cm (⅜ x 1in) rectangle
- Pink felt – one 1 x 2.5cm (⅜ x 1in) rectangle; four 1.5 x 1cm (⅝ x ⅜in) rectangles
- Selection of bright embroidery threads and buttons to decorate.
- Black, green and beige embroidery thread
- Toy stuffing
- 3mm (US D/3) crochet hook
- Removable stitch marker
- Tapestry needle
- Sewing needle

Garden:
- DK (light worsted) yarn:
  20g (¾oz) each of olive green, lime green and pale green (all shades of C)
- 20g (¾oz) of jade green (D)
- 6 x 1cm (2¼ x ⅜in) rectangle beige/cream felt

FAIRYTALE COTTAGE

Using a crocheted square as a base, make the cottage by working around each side of the square, building the walls using a simple treble crochet and changing colour for roof. The doors and windows are cut from snippets of felt and stitched on afterwards. I have made a simple granny square style front garden for the cottage to sit on but you could attach a little bit of ribbon to turn it into a cute hanging decoration, suitable for all dreamers of country cottages everywhere!

COTTAGE

Base:
Round 1: Using yarn A, 5ch, ss in first ch to join. 5ch (acts as 1tr and 2ch), [3tr in ring, 2ch] 3 times, 2tr in ring, ss in 3rd ch of t-ch to join. (4 groups of 3tr and 4 ch corners)
Rounds 2–3: Ss in next ch sp, 7ch (acts as 1tr and 4ch), *2tr in ch sp, 1tr in each tr, 2tr in next ch sp, 4ch; rep from * twice more, 2tr in ch sp, 3tr, 1 tr in same ch sp as 7ch , ss in 3rd ch of t-ch to join. (4 groups of 7[11]tr and 4 corners)

Walls:
Round 4: Work into chains and stitches as follows: pm, 3ch, 1tr in next ch, 11tr, *tr2tog 13tr; rep from *, tr2tog in last 2 chs, ss in 3rd ch of t-ch to join. (54 sts)
Rounds 5–7: 3ch, tr around, ss to 3rd ch of t-ch to join.
Fasten off.

Roof:
Round 8: Join yarn B at st marker, 3ch, tr(flo) around, ss to 3rd ch of t-ch to join. (54 sts)
Round 9: 3ch, tr around, ss in 3rd ch of t-ch to join. (54 sts)
Round 10: 3ch, *[tr2tog] 5 times, 1tr, [tr2tog] three times, 3tr, [tr2tog] 3 times*, 1tr, rep from * to *, ss in 3rd ch of t-ch to join. (32 sts)
Round 11: 3ch, [tr2tog, 1tr] across to last 2 sts, tr2tog. (16 sts)
Fill with toy stuffing.

Fold the roof in half lengthways along the front of the house, ss together to join.
Fasten off and weave in ends.

Chimney:
Rows 1: Using yarn A, 5ch, 1dc in 2nd ch from hook, 3dc, turn. (4 sts)
Rows 2–4: 1ch, dc across, turn. (4 sts)
Fasten off. Stitch sides together to form a small tube.

GRASS

Base ring: Using any shade of C, 5ch, join with ss to form a ring.
Round 1: 3ch, 2 tr in ring, *2ch, 3tr in ring; rep from * twice, htr in 3rd ch of t-ch to join.
Round 2: 3ch, 2tr in same ch sp, 1ch, [3tr in next ch sp, 2ch, 3tr in same ch sp, 1ch] twice, 3tr in next ch sp, join with htr in 3rd ch of t-ch.
Round 3: 3ch, 2tr in same ch sp, 1ch, [3tr in next ch sp, 1ch, 3tr in next ch sp, 2ch, 3tr in same ch sp, 1ch] twice, 3tr in next ch sp, join with htr in 3rd ch of t-ch.
Rounds 4–5: Rep Round 3 twice more, working [3tr, ch3, 3 tr] into each corner sp, 3tr, 1ch for each side sp and ending with htr to join. Change colour at each round or work all in one colour as preferred.
Fasten off. Weave in ends neatly.
At any corner of square, join yarn F and work in rows along one side as follows:
Rows 1–3: 3ch, 1tr in same ch sp, 1ch, [3tr in next ch sp, 1ch] 4 times, 1tr in corner, turn.
Fasten off.
This creates a rectangular base.

HEDGE

Made separately.

Using yarn D, 107ch.

Scallop edge: Ss in 2nd ch from hook, [miss 1 ch, 3tr in next ch, miss 1 ch, ss in next 2 chs] 21 times. (21 scallops)

Fasten off.

FINISHING

Stitch the cottage to the base across the join of the back garden and square front garden.

The cottage should sit just above the first round with the centre of the crochet square lining up with the front door.

Doors:

With cream embroidery thread, stitch the blue door piece of felt to the centre of the front of the cottage. Use a small button as a doorknob. Stitch the other pale pink door to the back of the house.

Windows:

Using black embroidery thread and needle, stitch the black squares of felt either side of front door. Stitch another square to the roof in the centre above the door and another square onto the back of the house.

Using the cream embroidery thread, stitch across the window squares twice horizontally and vertically criss-crossing in the centre to represent panes of glass.

Stitch one pink felt rectangle under each window to make a window box and stitch a rectangle on each side of window on roof to make shutters.

Path:

Using cream embroidery thread and needle, stitch the beige felt strip from the door down the length of the grass square at the front of the cottage. Place a st marker at each side of the path.

Hedge:

Using yarn F, starting at the left side st marker at path, stitch the hedge around each side of the base rectangle (grass and back garden), finishing at the other st marker at other side of path. Fasten off. Weave in all ends.

Using a little white sewing thread and a sewing needle, stitch a wisp of polyester toy stuffing to the top of chimney to look like smoke.

Embroidery:

See pages 122–123 for details of embroidery stitches. Using bright pink yarn, make small French knots around door as little roses. With green yarn make small straight stitch leaves between roses.

Abbreviations

ch	chain
ch sp	chain space
dc	double crochet
dc2tog	double crochet two sts together
flo	front loop only
htr	half treble
pm	place marker
rep	repeat
ss	slip stitch
st(s)	stitch(es)
tr2tog	treble two sts together
t-ch	turning chain
tr	treble

Skill level: ★★★

Size

19cm (7½in)

You will need

- DK (light worsted) yarn:
  20g (¾oz) each of medium grey (A),
  pale grey (B) and dark grey (C)
  10g (⅜oz) each of blue (D) and
  green (E)
  Small amount of brown, lime green,
  pink and orange
- 3mm (US D/3) crochet hook
- Removable stitch marker
- Tapestry needle
- Toy stuffing
- Bamboo skewers – two 12cm
  (4¾in) lengths
- Medium gauge wire – 10cm
  (4in) length

Abbreviations

blo	back loop only
ch	chain
ch sp	chain space
dc	double crochet
flo	front loop only
pm	place marker
rep	repeat
ss	slip stitch
st(s)	stitch(es)
t-ch	turning chain
tr	treble
yrh	yarn round hook

Special abbreviation

3tr cluster – *yrh, insert hook in the required stitch, yrh again and draw a loop through. Yrh, draw through 2 of the loops, leaving 2 loops on hook; rep from * twice more ending with 4 loops on hook, yrh and draw through all the loops on the hook to complete cluster.

THE ENCHANTED WISHING WELL

This wishing well makes a magical scene setter to add into other fairytale scenes in this book. Some simple clusters make the roof tiles and the stone walls of the well look more realistic. I have used bamboo skewers and wire to add the roof supports and handle.

ROOF

This is made in two pieces.

Outer roof:

Worked from top down.

Base ring: Using yarn A, 2ch, 7dc in 2nd ch from hook, ss in first dc to join. (7 sts)

Rounds 1–3: Pm, dc around. (7 sts)

Cluster pattern:

Round 4: 3ch, 3tr cluster in base of ch, 1ch, [3tr cluster in next st, 1ch] 6 times, ss in 3rd ch of t-ch to join. (7 clusters)

Round 5: 3ch, *3tr cluster in ch sp, 1ch; rep from * around, ss in 3rd ch of t-ch to join. (7 clusters)

Round 6: 3ch, 3tr cluster, 1ch in each cluster and ch sp of Round 5. (14 clusters)

Round 7: 3ch, miss first ch sp, *3tr cluster in next st (at top of cluster in Round 6), 1ch, [3tr cluster in ch sp, 1ch, 3tr cluster in cluster, 1ch]; rep from * 6 times, 3tr cluster in ch sp, 3tr cluster in cluster, ss in 3rd ch of t-ch to join. (20 clusters)

Rounds 7–8: 3ch, 3tr cluster in each ch sp around. (20 clusters)

Round 9: 1ch, 1dc in each cluster and ch sp around, ss in first dc to join. (40 sts)

Fasten off.

Roof lining:

Working from top down.

Base ring: Using yarn A, 2ch, 6dc in 2nd ch from hook, ss in first dc to join. (6 sts)

Rounds 1–3: Pm, dc around. (6 sts)

Round 4: 2dc in each st around. (12 sts)

Rounds 5–8: Dc around. (12 sts)

Round 9: 2dc in each st around. (24 sts)

Round 10: Dc around. (24 sts)

Round 11: [2dc in next st, 1dc] 12 times. (36 sts)

Round 12: [2dc in next st, 5dc] 6 times. (42 sts)

Round 13: Dc around. (42 sts)

Fasten off.

WELL

Worked from the base up.

Base ring: Using yarn B, 5ch, ss in first ch to make a ring.

Round 1: 3ch, 13tr in ring, ss in 3rd ch of t-ch to join. (14 sts)

Round 2: 3ch, 1tr in base of ch, 2tr in each st a round. (28 sts)

Round 3: 1ch, dc (blo) around. (28 sts)

Walls:

Round 4: 3ch, 3tr cluster in base of ch, 2ch, [miss next st, 3tr cluster in next st, 2ch] 13 times, ss in 3rd ch of t-ch to join. (14 clusters)

Fasten off.

Join yarn C in any ch sp.

Round 5: 3ch, 3tr cluster in same ch sp, 2ch, 3tr cluster, 2ch in each ch sp around ss to 3rd ch of t-ch to join. (14 clusters)

Fasten off.

Round 6: Join yarn A to any ch sp, rep Round 5. (14 clusters)

Fasten off.

Round 7: Join yarn B to any ch sp, rep Round 5.

Rounds 8–11: Ss in next ch sp, rep Round 5. (14 clusters)

Round 9: Work in both the ch sp and cluster as follows: 3ch, *2tr(flo), 2tr(flo) in next st; rep from * to end, ss in 3rd ch of t-ch to join. (41 sts)

Fasten off.

Round 10: Join yarn A, 1ch, dc(blo) around, ss in first dc to join. (41 sts)

Fasten off.

Put some toy stuffing into base of well.

Grass:

Attach yarn E to any outside loop of Round 2 (base of well) 3ch, 1tr in base of ch, 2tr in each outside loop around, ss in 3rd ch of t-ch to join. (56 sts)

Fasten off.

Water in well:

Base ring: Using yarn D, 5ch, ss in first ch to join.

Round 1: 3ch, 13tr in ring, ss in 3rd ch of t-ch to join. (14 sts)

Round 2: 1ch, 2dc in each st around, ss in first dc to join. (28 sts)

Fasten off.

Round 3: Join yarn A to the blo, 3ch, 1tr (blo) in each st around. (28 sts)

Fasten off.

WELL HANDLE

With the 10cm (4in) length of wire, bend at right angle at approximately 7cm (2¾in) using pliers. Bend remaining wire into a spiral.

Place the two bamboo skewers parallel to each other about 5cm (2in) apart. About 4cm from each end, place the wire handle across the two uprights, in a H shape.

Using brown yarn, wind around the point where the uprights and wire handle cross. Keep winding yarn around until the pieces are held securely together, stitch through the yarn occasionally as you work. Once the handle is securely attached in place, wrap yarn round each piece until fully covered.

Insert the upright ends into the base of the well and stitch in place securely, stitching through wrapped yarn on skewers as much as possible to hold it firmly in place. At other end of uprights sew the uprights to the inside of the outer roof.

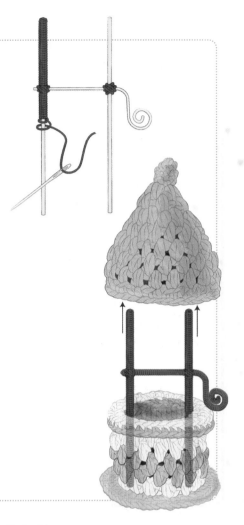

FINISHING

Place the water into the top of the well, on top of the toy stuffing. Cover the ends of uprights of handle (see box above) and, using yarn E, stitch Round 3 to the inside of the top of well to make a lining at the top of the well and water inside the well.

Roof:

Put roof lining section up inside outer section of roof and, using tail of yarn A, stitch inside to make the lining cover the ends of the handle uprights as you sew.

Embroidery:

See pages 122–123 for details of embroidery stitches. Use pink, orange and lime green yarn to embroider a simple chain stitch flower onto the side of the well, just above the grass as follows: Using lime green make a line of 4 or 5 chain stitches moving upwards at a slight angle as the stem. At either side of line, make two chain stitches to look like leaves.

Using the orange yarn, make a French knot above the line of green for the centre of the flower. Using pink yarn, work daisy stitch around the French knot to make the petals.

Techniques

In this section, we explain how to master the simple crochet, sewing and construction techniques that you need to make the projects in this book.

BASIC CROCHET TECHNIQUES

Holding the hook

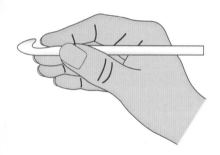

Pick up your hook as though you are picking up a pen or pencil. Keeping the hook held loosely between your fingers and thumb, turn your hand so that the palm is facing up and the hook is balanced in your hand and resting in the space between your index finger and your thumb.

Holding the yarn

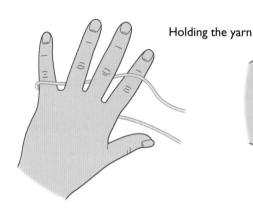

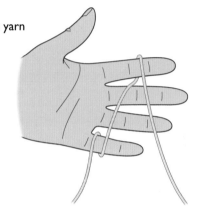

1. Pick up the yarn with your little finger in the opposite hand to your hook, with your palm facing upwards and with the short end in front. Turn your hand to face downwards, with the yarn on top of your index finger and under the other two fingers and wrapped right around the little finger, as shown above.

2. Turn your hand to face you, ready to hold the work in your middle finger and thumb. Keeping your index finger only at a slight curve, hold the work or the slip knot using the same hand, between your middle finger and your thumb and just below the crochet hook and loop/s on the hook.

Making a slip knot

The simplest way is to make a circle with the yarn, so that the loop is facing downwards.

1. In one hand hold the circle at the top where the yarn crosses, and let the tail drop down at the back so that it falls across the centre of the loop. With your free hand or the tip of a crochet hook, pull a loop through the circle.

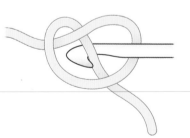

2. Put the hook into the loop and pull gently so that it forms a loose loop on the hook.

Yarn round hook (yrh)

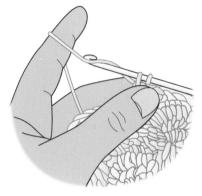

To create a stitch, catch the yarn from behind with the hook pointing upwards. As you gently pull the yarn through the loop on the hook, turn the hook so it faces downwards and slide the yarn through the loop. The loop on the hook should be kept loose enough for the hook to slide through easily.

Magic ring

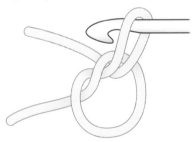

This is useful starting technique if you do not want a visible hole in the centre of your round. Loop the yarn around your finger, insert the hook through the ring, yarn over hook and pull through the ring to make the first chain. Work the number of stitches required into the ring and then pull the end to tighten the centre ring.

Chain (ch)

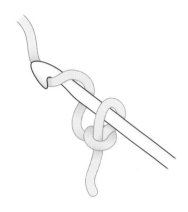

1. Using the hook, wrap the yarn round the hook ready to pull it through the loop on the hook.

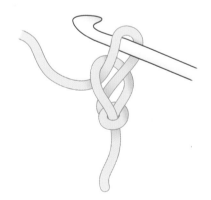

2. Pull through, creating a new loop on the hook. Continue in this way to create a chain of the required length.

Chain ring

If you are crocheting a round shape, one way of starting off is by crocheting a number of chains following the instructions in your pattern, and then joining them into a circle.

1. To join the chain into a circle, insert the crochet hook into the first chain that you made (not into the slip knot), yarn round hook.

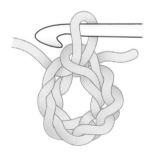

2. Pull the yarn through the chain and through the loop on your hook at the same time, thereby creating a slip stitch and forming a circle. You now have a chain ring ready to work stitches into as instructed in the pattern.

Chain space (ch sp)

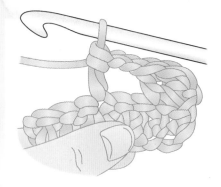

1. A chain space is the space that has been made under a chain in the previous round or row, and falls in between other stitches.

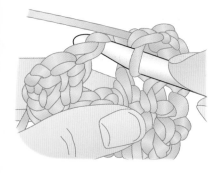

2. Stitches into a chain space are made directly into the hole created under the chain and not into the chain stitches themselves.

Making rounds

When working in rounds the work is not turned, so you are always working from one side. Depending on the pattern you are working, a 'round' can be square. Start each round by making one or more chains to create the height you need for the stitch you are working:

Double crochet = 1 chain

Half treble = 2 chain

Treble = 3 chain

Work the required stitches to complete the round. At the end of the round, slip stitch into the top of the chain to close the round.

If you work in a spiral you do not need a turning chain. After completing your base ring, place a stitch marker in the first stitch and then continue to crochet around. When you have made a round and reached the point where the stitch marker is, work this stitch, take out the stitch marker from the previous round and put it back into the first stitch of the new round. A safety pin or piece of yarn in a contrasting colour is a good stitch marker.

Making rows

When making straight rows you turn the work at the end of each row and make a turning chain to create the height you need for the stitch you are working with, as for Making rounds.

Slip stitch (ss)

A slip stitch doesn't create any height and is often used as the last stitch to create a smooth and even round or row.

1. To make a slip stitch: first put the hook through the work, yarn round hook.

2. Pull the yarn through both the work and through the loop on the hook at the same time, so you will have one loop on the hook.

Working into top of stitch

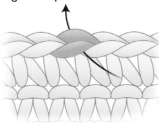

Unless otherwise directed, insert the hook under both of the two loops on top of the stitch – this is the standard technique.

Working into front loop of stitch (flo)

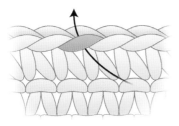

To work into the front loop of a stitch, pick up the front loop from underneath at the front of the work.

Working into back loop of stitch (blo)

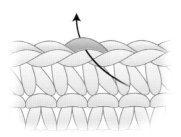

To work into the back loop of the stitch, insert the hook between the front and the back loop, picking up the back loop from the front of the work.

Double crochet (dc)

1. Insert the hook into your work, yarn round hook and pull the yarn through the work only. You will then have two loops on the hook.

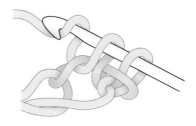

2. Yarn round hook again and pull through the two loops on the hook. You will then have one loop on the hook.

Joining new yarn

If using double crochet to join in a new yarn, insert the hook as normal into the stitch, using the original yarn, and pull a loop through. Drop the old yarn and pick up the new yarn. Wrap the new yarn round the hook and pull it through the two loops on the hook.

Half treble (htr)

1. Before inserting the hook into the work, wrap the yarn round the hook and put the hook through the work with the yarn wrapped around.

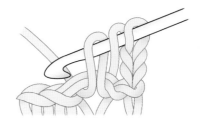

2. Yarn round hook again and pull through the first loop on the hook. You now have three loops on the hook.

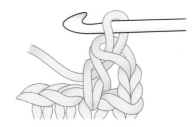

3. Yarn round hook and pull the yarn through all three loops. You will be left with one loop on the hook.

Treble (tr)

1. Before inserting the hook into the work, wrap the yarn round the hook. Put the hook through the work with the yarn wrapped around, yarn round hook again and pull through the first loop on the hook. You now have three loops on the hook.

2. Yarn round hook again, pull the yarn through the first two loops on the hook. You now have two loops on the hook.

3. Pull the yarn through two loops again. You will be left with one loop on the hook.

Cluster (CL)

Working two or more part stitches and taking them together at the top to make one stitch gives a cluster in a stitch pattern or a decrease when working a fabric. The example shows making a cluster by taking three trebles (3tr cluster) together.

Leaving the last loop of each stitch on the hook, work a treble into each of the next three stitches, thus making four loops on the hook. Yarn round hook and pull through all four loops to join the stitches together at the top and make one loop on the hook.

Increasing

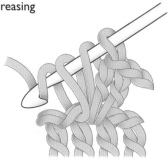

Make two or three stitches into one stitch or space from the previous row. The illustration shows a two-stitch treble increase being made.

Blocking

Crochet can tend to curl so to make flat pieces stay flat you may need to block them. Pin the piece out to the correct size and shape on the ironing board, then press or steam gently (depending on the type of yarn) and allow to dry completely.

Decreasing

You can decrease by either missing the next stitch and continuing to crochet, or by crocheting two or more stitches together. The basic technique for crocheting stitches together is the same, no matter which stitch you are using. The following examples show dc2tog, tr3tog and htr2tog.

Double crochet two stitches together (dc2tog)

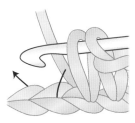

1. Insert the hook into your work, yarn round hook and pull the yarn through the work. You will then have two loops on the hook.

2. Yarn round hook again and pull through the two loops on the hook. You will then have one loop on the hook.

Treble three stitches together (tr3tog)

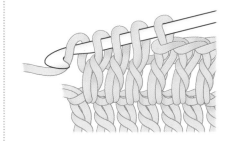

Work a treble into each of the next three stitches as normal, but leave the last loop of each stitch on the hook so you finish with four loops on the hook. Yarn round hook and pull the yarn through all four stitches on the hook to join them together. You will finish with one loop on the hook.

Half treble two stitches together (htr2tog)

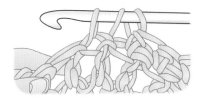

1. Yarn round hook, insert hook into next stitch, yarn round hook, draw yarn through. You now have three loops on the hook.

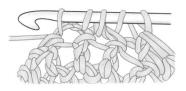

2. Yarn round hook, insert hook into next stitch, yarn round hook, draw yarn through. This leaves five loops on the hook.

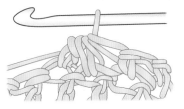

3. Draw yarn through all five loops on the hook. You will then have one loop on the hook.

BASIC SEWING TECHNIQUES

Running stitch

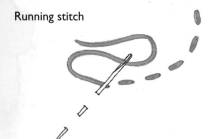

Work from right to left. Secure the thread with a couple of small stitches, and then make several small stitches by bringing the needle up and back down through the crochet fabric several times along the stitching line. Pull the needle through and repeat. Try to keep the stitches and the spaces between them the same size.

Star stitch

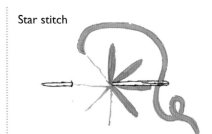

Work a series of straight stitches radiating out from the centre of a circle to create a star shape. If you wish, you can further embellish this stitch by working a French knot at the tip of each point of the star.

Chain stitch

Bring the needle out at the start of the stitching line. Re-insert it at the same point and bring it out a short distance away, looping the thread around the needle tip. Pull the thread through. For the next stitch insert the needle right next to where it last emerged, just inside the loop of the previous chain, and bring it out a short distance away, again looping the thread around the needle tip. Fasten off at the end of the chain by taking a small vertical stitch across the bottom of the loop.

Daisy stitch

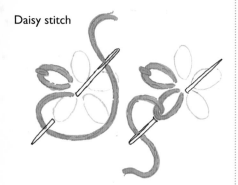

Work a single chain, as for chain stitch, but fasten it by taking a small vertical stitch across the bottom of the loop. Make more single chains in a circle to create the daisy.

Backstitch

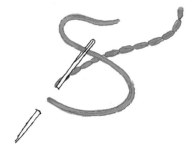

Work from right to left. Bring the needle up from the back of the fabric, one stitch length to the left of the end of the stitching line. Insert it one stitch length to the right, at the very end of the stitching line, and bring it up again one stitch length in front of the point from which it first emerged. Pull the thread through. To begin the next stitch, insert the needle at the left-hand end of the previous stitch. Continue to the end.

French knot

Bring the needle up from the back of the fabric to the front. Wrap the thread two or three times around the tip of the needle, then reinsert the needle at the point where it first emerged, holding the wrapped threads with the thumbnail of your non-stitching hand, and pull the needle all the way through. The wraps will form a knot on the surface of the fabric.

Sewing on a bead

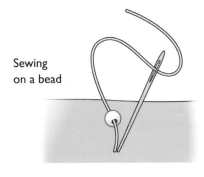

Bring the thread up through the fabric then thread on the bead. Take the thread over the bead and back down through the fabric.

Sewing on a button

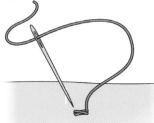

1. Mark the place where you want the button to go. Push the needle up from the back of the fabric and sew a few stitches over and over in this place.

2. Now bring the needle up through one of the holes in the button. Push the needle back down through the second hole and through the fabric. Bring it back up through the first hole. Repeat this five or six times. If there are four holes in the button, use all four of them to make a cross pattern. Make sure that you keep the stitches close together under the middle of the button.

Blanket stitch

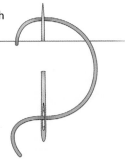

1. Bring the needle through to the front at the edge of the fabric. Push the needle back through the fabric a short distance from the edge and loop the thread under the needle at the edge of the fabric. Pull the needle and thread through to make the first stitch.

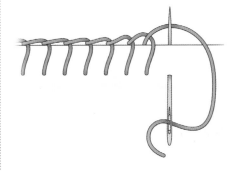

2. Make another stitch to the right of this and again loop the thread under the needle. Continue along the fabric and finish with a few small stitches or a knot on the underside.

Making a pompom

1. Decide the diameter of the finished pompom and cut two pieces of stiff card the same diameter. Draw a smaller circle exactly in the middle of each and cut out to make two rings.

2. Hold the two rings together and wrap the yarn around through the centre hole, wrapping closely but not too tightly or it will be difficult to cut. When the rings have lots of layers of yarn, carefully push the point of a pair of scissors between the layers of card, and snip through the yarn all around the ring.

3. Thread a length of yarn between the card layers and knot tightly. Pull off the card rings and fluff up the pompom. Trim any straggly ends with scissors to make a neat ball. For a very small pompom, just wrap the yarn about 60 times around a small square of card the size of the pompom, carefully slide the wraps off, tie in the middle, and then fluff up and trim off any ends.

MAKING FACES

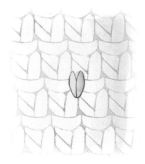

1. Make two straight stitches (see page 122) using a suitable yarn or embroidery thread colour to make a V shape eye pupil.

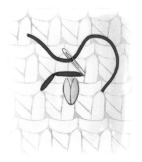

2. Add three backstitches (see page 122) in a slight curve over the pupil, using black or brown thread or yarn, to create the eyelid shape.

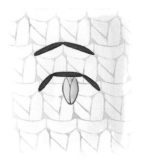

3. Add two backstitches above the eye in black or brown thread or yarn to create an eyebrow.

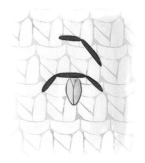

4. If you angle the eyebrow stitches into the centre of the face it gives an angry look.

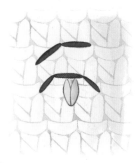

5. If you angle the eyebrow stitches in the other direction, toward the sides of the face, it gives a sad look.

6. For a sleepy eye, don't make a pupil and make the three stitches in step 2 curve the other way. Add eyelashes at the outer corners.

7. To create the mouth, make two backstitches in red embroidery thread, giving them a slight curve.

8. You can add a cross stitch over the top in the same colour for a cute cupid-bow look.

MAKING WIRE ARMS AND LEGS

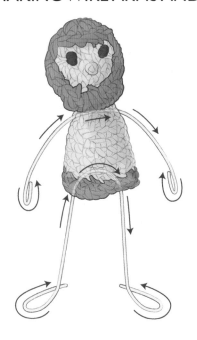

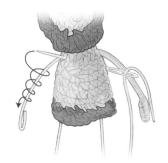

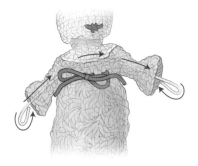

2. Push a darning needle threaded with the correct colour yarn (see project) through the body near to where the wire emerges. Leaving the end concealed inside, wrap the yarn around continuously to cover the wire fully from body to loop. Stitch around and through the centre of the loop until it is fully covered and then thread the darning needle back through a few wraps and snip off the yarn end close to the limb.

3. If the model's clothing has sleeves, push the arm wire into the first sleeve, through the body and out through the second sleeve. Bend each end of wire over by about 1 cm (⅜in) to make hand loops. Using the threaded darning needle, stitch through the first hand loop, wrap the yarn around the loop and continue to wrap the wire up to the sleeve. Stitch up inside the sleeve, through the body and down the inside of the second sleeve. Repeat the wrapping around wire down to the second wire loop hand as before until the arm and hand are fully covered.

1. For the arms, push a length of wire through the body in the required position and fold the ends over into loops to make the hands. For the legs, curve a longer length of wire into a U shape and push through the base of the body. Twist the ends into a loop to make the feet. If the model needs to stand, for stability make bigger loops, leaving a short spur of wire at the back.

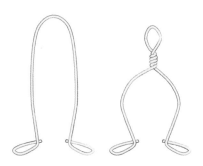

4. Some models need some wire support from the legs inside the body. Bend a 22cm (8in) length of wire into a U shape and twist the ends into loops to make the feet. Then twist at the top to make a loop as shown.

5. Push each wire leg through the leg-hole in the bottom part of the clothing, or through the skirt base, and into the correct position. Use the tail of yarn from the crochet to stitch the ends of leg-holes tightly around wires. Push the top of the wire into the stuffed body and then stitch the parts together as described in the project.

Tip

If you are inserting the legs through a skirt base instead of into trousers, don't bend the foot loops until after the legs are in position.

MAKING TREE BASES

1. Place several wires together into a bundle and wrap a short length of wire tightly round at the bottom to make a trunk. Pull the ends of the wire apart at the top to start forming branches. Twist smaller lengths of wire onto the main wires for more tree branches. Thread a tapestry needle with brown DK and stitch through at the bottom of the trunk to attach. Draw the yarn through and stitch round the end of the trunk several times. Wrap the yarn around the trunk and branches until there are no gaps of wire left visible. Stitch through at the end and fasten off.

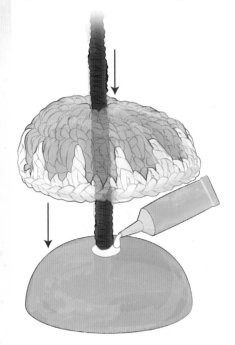

2. Roll a piece of clay into a ball shape and press down onto a tray or plate to flatten a base on one side. Mould the top into a rounded dome shape. Push the end of the trunk into clay to a depth of about 1.5cm (⅝in) and then take out, leaving a trunk-sized hole, and set the clay aside to dry for 24 hours. When dry, push the trunk through the centre of the crochet grass (see instructions in the project). Put a drop of glue into the hole in the base, then insert the tree trunk and push down firmly.

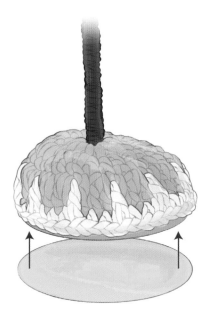

3. Smooth the grass over the top and leave until the glue is fully dry. When dry, place the felt circle under the base and stitch the felt to the grass all around the edge matching yarn or thread.

CROCHET STITCH CONVERSION CHART

Crochet stitches are worked in the same way in both the UK and the USA, but the stitch names are not the same and identical names are used for different stitches. Below is a list of the UK terms used in this book, and the equivalent US terms.

UK TERM	US TERM
double crochet (dc)	single crochet (sc)
half treble (htr)	half double crochet (hdc)
treble (tr)	double crochet (dc)
double treble (dtr)	treble (tr)
triple treble (trtr)	double treble (dtr)
quadruple treble (qtr)	triple treble (trtr)
yarn round hook (yrh)	yarn over hook (yoh)

INDEX

SUPPLIERS

UK

Deramores
Online store only
Tel: 0800 488 0708
www.deramores.com

John Lewis
Retail stores and online
www.johnlewis.com
Telephone numbers of local stores on website
Tel: 03456 049049

The Wool Bar
15 Warwick Street
Worthing
West Sussex BN11 3DF
Tel: 01903 235445
www.thewoolbar.co.uk

Accessories:

The Fabric Shop Ltd
55 Chapel Road
Worthing
West Sussex BN11 1EF
www.thefabricshops.co.uk

Beads Unlimited
Online and at The Brighton Bead Shop.
21 Sydney Street.
Brighton.
East Sussex BN1 4EN
www.beadsunlimited.co.uk

Duttons for Buttons
Stores in Harrogate, Ilkley and York and online
www.duttonsforbuttons.co.uk

USA

Knitting Fever Inc.
PO Box 336
315 Bayview Avenue
Amityville, NY 11701
www.knittingfever.com

Lion Brand Yarns
Tel: +1 800 258 YARN (9276)
Online sales and store locator on website
www.lionbrand.com

Westminster Fibers
165 Ledge Street
Nashua, NH 03060
Tel: +1 800 445 9276
www.westminsterfibers.com

Accessories:

A.C. Moore
Stores nationwide
Tel: +1 888 226 6673
www.acmoore.com

Hobby Lobby
Online store and stores nationwide
www.hobbylobby.com

Michaels
Stores nationwide
Tel: +1 800 642 4235
www.michaels.com

Canada

Diamond Yarn
155 Martin Ross Avenue, Unit 3
Toronto, ON
M3J 2L9
Tel: +1 416 736 6111
www.diamondyarn.com

Westminster Fibers
10 Roybridge Gate, Suite 200
Vaughn, ON
L4H 3MB
Tel: +1 800 263 2354
www.westminsterfibers.com

Australia

Black Sheep Wool 'n' Wares
Tel: +61 (0)2 6779 1196
www.blacksheepwool.com.au

Creative Images Crafts
PO Box 106
Hastings
VIC 3915
Tel: +61 (0)3 5979 1555

ACKNOWLEDGEMENTS

Writing this book has been such an amazing new experience for me and I am in no doubt that it could not have happened at all without the help, support, creativity and expertise of many people. I thank them all but can only mention a few here.

I would like to say a huge thank you to Penny Craig, Carmel Edmonds and the lovely people at CICO books for taking a leap of faith in me and commissioning this book, for all their hard work in bringing it into print and for being so creative and inventive. Thank you for Marie Clayton's super editing and Zoe Clements' technical skills and crochet wizardry, and for their kind patience in wrestling my airy-fairy making techniques into accurate patterns and instructions.

To my friends, Fiona Hesford, for supporting me and inspiring me into thinking I could do it, and Karen Mayger, for your incredible crochet skills, pattern checking and supporting me so brilliantly at such a difficult time in your own life.

Thank you to my pal Caroline Wilbor at The Wool Bar in Worthing, for all your kind words of encouragement and for supplying me with lovely yarns when my stash could not cope – and for the delicious coffees.

I want to thank my husband Phil and my three daughters for the love and support, the cups of tea and for tolerating a house full of yarn all the time. Thank you for putting up with it all and for not rolling your eyes too much, girls! I love you all very much.

Finally, I want to say thank you to my mum and dad, both now gone but still loved and missed every day; this book is for you, Joan and John.